"IT'S ONLY a Tattoo"

AND OTHER MYTHS TEENS BELIEVE

"IT'S ONLY a Tattoo"

AND OTHER MYTHS TEENS BELIEVE

RON LUCE

Life Journey® is an imprint of
Cook Communications Ministries, Colorado Springs, CO 80918
Cook Communications, Paris, Ontario
Kingsway Communications, Eastbourne, England

"IT'S ONLY A TATTOO" AND OTHER MYTHS TEENS BELIEVE
© Copyright 2006 by Ron Luce

First printing 2006
Printed in the United States of America
        1 2 3 4 5 6 7 8 9 10 Printing/Year 11 10 09 08 07 06

Cover Design: Identity Design
Interior Design: Sandy Flewelling/TrueBlue Design

Ron Luce is the founder and president of Teen Mania Ministries.

Library of Congress Control Number: 2005938329

ISBN: 0-78144-378-4

dedication

This book is dedicated to parents of teenagers who are desperately trying their best to raise virtuous children. And to teenagers who are passionately pursuing God's presence in their lives to change the world.

acknowledgements

Eight years ago my wife Katie and I formulated the principles you are about to read. Over these eight years of raising our children into their teenage years and witnessing the major moral shifting of society, we have refined these principles.

I want to thank the original crew who helped with this book: Joni Jones, the editor; and the young ladies in my office: Alece Ronzino, Kimberly Houle, Beth McNinch, Charlene Garrett, Sarah Baltzley, Mica Marley, and Dawn Stauffer who worked many hours typing it. I also want to express appreciation to Michelle Franzen, who was my executive assistant; she put up with many things during the process of this book.

I would also like to thank the team who worked on this new edition. Thank you to Janet Lee, who has worked long and hard on this, as well as Sharron Jackson, Doug Mauss, and the rest of the Cook Communications team.

Our prayer is that this book will help parents to help their teens—and ultimately help a generation.

contents

"It's Only a Tattoo" and Other Myths Teens Believe:
A Parent's Response Handbook

introduction

Raising teenagers today is not the same as it was even 20 years ago. Our society has changed, pressures have changed, temptations have changed, peer pressure has changed—and it has all affected our families. So many young people struggle to figure out who they are and who they are supposed to be, and their parents struggle to figure out how to handle new and different challenges with their teens.

Traveling over the years and speaking to hundreds of thousands of teenagers, I have spent countless hours listening to them share about their families, their struggles, and their challenges. After hearing how parents deal with those challenges, I have prepared this book to offer insight regarding the problems that most commonly face your young person. It is specifically designed to help you break through a number of problem and crisis areas.

You can read through the whole book, or you can use it as a reference manual when you face problem situations. If you read through the whole thing, you will probably prevent a lot of difficult circumstances before they occur. This book is a "how-to" guide, helping you as a parent get through the difficult situations your parents probably never faced when you were a teenager. It gives you suggestions of steps to take, discusses the principles behind those steps, and offers ideas that will help you communicate them to your young person.

You will read comments from teens about how they wish their parents would handle the struggles they face. Statistics and comments from experts in the field will provide insight as to why certain problems target certain kids. But most importantly, you will be |given a biblical understanding of how to approach various issues.

If you as a parent were to come to me, look me in the eye, and tell me about your young person in one of these situations, what you are about to read is exactly what I would say to you. Since it is impossible to meet one-on-one with the parents of the hundreds of thousands of teens I meet every year, I believe the spiritual principles in this book will help you get through the crises you face. Picture yourself coming into my office to talk about your particular teen's situations or me coming to your home as you read this book to find specific answers to the challenges you are facing. God bless you in your relationship with your teenager!

family

He's finally here! That cuddly, little infant you anxiously awaited for nine long months has arrived. You're excited about the new addition to your family. You feed your baby, clothe your baby, and change your baby's diapers. You take care of your baby's every need. As your little one grows up, you answer all his questions, teach him about life, help him with spelling, and take him to football practice, piano lessons, and after-school activities.

Then, something happens. At 12 or 13 years old, your teen thinks he has the right and the wisdom to make his own decisions. Most parents respond, "As long as you are in my house, you are going to do it my way!" It becomes a perpetual argument in the home.

You ask him questions, and his only response is, "I don't know." You know there is a wall , but how can you get through the rebellion and the lies?

chapter 1 — Communication: Getting Through to Your Teen

there's a wall

You ask your teen what is going on in school and with friends. "What do you want to know my business for? Why are you so nosy?" You realize there is not just a gap, but a wall keeping you from getting into your teen's world.

> "I feel like there is a wall between me and my parents. They just don't understand how I feel. We have talked about it, and we get along a little better, but things just aren't the way I wish they would be."

> "I wish they just would have said they will love and accept me no matter what I choose to do or what friends I have."

As you can see, situations like this not only cause a lot of hurt, but also build a huge barrier. According to Jay Kesler, the top ten mistakes parents make with their children are to say:

1. *Do as I say, not as I do.*
2. *I'm the adult. I'm right.*
3. *Because I said so, that's why.*
4. *You want to be what?*
5. *This room's a pigsty.*
6. *Can't you do anything right?*
7. *Where did you find them?*
8. *You did what?*
9. *Do you mind if we talk about something else?*
10. *I'm kind of busy right now. Could you come back later?* [1]

When parents have finally discovered a wall exists and an entirely different life is on the other side, they find it seemingly impossible to break through. Your teen has taken years to build that wall out of brick and stone and does not want to tear it down quickly.

To break through the walls of your relationship, here are a couple of principles to follow:

Own your mistakes. Most walls begin to go up when something has been said or done, either one time or on a number of occasions, that has caused hurt, and no effort has been made to deal with that hurt. It is impossible to live without getting hurt by someone. Relationships are made out of two or more emotionally complex individuals. The goal is not to avoid the hurt, but to know how to deal with an offense when there is one. Think back through situations that may have caused your teen pain or turmoil: divorce, words exchanged in an argument, or repeated words of accusation or insult. As parents, we must take responsibility to find these barriers and tear them down.

When you listen, the person you're listening to feels like you care enough to really tune in.

> **"I wish that my parents would admit
> that sometimes they are at fault too."**

Once you've identified those areas of possible hurt, go to your teen and ask her to forgive you for the specifics that may have caused pain. Don't make a blanket statement such as, "I'm sorry for anything I may have done . . . " Make sure you back up your apology by changing your vernacular or your actions in a certain area to show her you meant it. As you begin to ask for forgiveness, her heart will begin to soften.

Really listen to your kids. James 1:19 says, ". . . be quick to listen, slow to speak and slow to become angry." Most of us are slow to listen, quick to speak, and quicker to get angry. If you want to really find out what is going on with your teen, begin to listen to her.

> **"They should have tried to listen.
> I don't even try anymore."**

> **"They wouldn't listen; they overreacted."**

> **"My parents would be the greatest parents
> in the world if they didn't ask me to be honest
> about my feelings and then get totally upset
> if I express my true feelings."**

> **"I wish that my parents would stop talking and
> listen to what I have to say. I want to tell them so
> much, but they never stop to listen to me."**

Make a habit of listening—not just when you ask, "What's going on in your life?" but when she is sharing stories from school or other things that may seem unimportant to you. Repeat in your

FAMILY

Photo © Stockbyte

mind what she says in order to focus on her. Tune in to the feelings behind the words. "The words of a man's mouth are deep waters" (Prov. 18:4a). Behind the words is a person trying to express something really deep, if you'll only listen.

When you listen, the person you're listening to feels like you care enough to really tune in. You don't even have to say you care—she can tell you do because you listen, and in turn, that will make your teen more inclined to hear your words as well. An unspoken reciprocity makes a person feel obligated to listen to you after you have taken the time to truly hear her. Don't try to make your teen feel obligated. Wait for her to *want* to, and you'll begin to see the walls break down.

Another teen said:

> "I made a mistake with a boy and my parents drilled it out of me. Then they told me they were going to talk to him and his parents. That made me feel like I could never trust them with anything again."

As you are listening, be careful how you react to what you hear. Your reaction will determine whether your teen will trust you in the future.

Most teens feel lonely because they don't know their own parents. They sleep under the same roof with strangers every night. The walls in your relationship have been up long enough. Break them down and get to know each other once again. By admitting your failures, asking forgiveness, really listening, and sharing your heart when you talk, you'll be amazed at how restoration will happen in your relationship.

he fights me about everything

> "I have a rebellious attitude, and every
> time my parents tell me I do, it makes
> me even more rebellious."

> "My parents say I am rebellious, but I don't
> think I am half as bad as I could be. Personally,
> I think that if they only took a look at how they
> acted when they were younger, they would
> realize how much worse I could be."

> "Understand why I'm rebellious or selfish,
> and help me to change in a way that
> won't make me want to rebel more."

In dealing with rebellion, we first need to ask ourselves a couple of questions.

How frequent and intense is the rebellion?

According to Kathleen McCoy, Ph.D., "Normal rebellion is sporadic. There are moments of sweetness, calm, and cooperation between outbursts. If, on the other hand, rebellion is constant and intense, this can be a sign of underlying emotional problems." [2]

Is this a drastic behavior change?

Normal rebellious behavior develops over time, but if it is drastic—where behavior is completely reverse of what it was—this may be a sign of a deeper problem.

Why do teenagers have such a propensity for rebellion? Dr. James Dobson attributes it to two main reasons. One is hormonal in origin. Because of hormonal changes, both males and females may be easily set off. The other is social. The peer group has become more important than anything else, and the pressures to be their own person and identify with a generation has become much more intense than ever before in their lives.[3]

In Josh McDowell's *Handbook on Counseling Youth*, McDowell gives several causes for rebellion: poor relationship with parents, no effort to communicate, a need for control, a lack of boundaries and expectations, an expression of anger and aggression, and the absence of an honest, vulnerable model.[4]

Rebellion has different stages. Some are just minor and take place when teens are self-centered or desire independence. Such teens commonly exhort, "I want my own way!"

Further stages of rebellion occur when teens have an emotionless attitude of resistance and a hardened heart: "I don't care what you say or do, I'm going to do my own thing!"

Let's look at a few principles that will help you understand where your young person is coming from.

Rules without relationship equal rebellion. As one young lady said, "One of the worst things my parents have done is give me a 'no' answer without explaining why." When asked about a rule, most parents never explain the reason for it. "Because I say so, that is why!" Teens want to know the why of rules and understand the reasons behind them.

Just because your young person wants to make his own decisions in life doesn't mean he is rebellious—it means he is starting to grow up!

Your young person needs to know the person who is implementing the rules. When your teen feels forced to obey a rule but doesn't believe that you know or care about him, it produces a rebellious attitude.

Your young person wants to be able to make some of his own decisions. Even though you may still see him as young and not knowing what to do or where to go, your teen sees himself as quite skilled in life and wants to have some control. Your teen needs to be able to say, "I made this decision, and I realize it was a good decision." If you make all the decisions while your child lives under your roof, he will never understand and learn how to make his own decisions.

A teen's desire for responsibility can be perceived as rebellion. But just because your young person wants to make his own decisions in life doesn't mean he is rebellious—it means he is starting to grow up! Start out with small decisions. The goal is getting him to make all his decisions before leaving home.

What decisions do you make for your young person and what decisions do you let him make? That is between you and God. Pray and find out from the Lord. By the time he is 18, your young person should be weaned from having all his decisions made for him. He should be able to make decisions about his life in a mature, responsible way.

It is much better for him to make bad decisions under your protective umbrella, where you can go back and talk about the failure and how to do it right the next time, than for him to leave home and make all wrong decisions.

just tell me the truth

**"I find myself lying to my parents.
I wish that lying wasn't the only way
we could keep things cool between us."**

**"I wish my parents would say that being honest
and getting in trouble are more important than
lying and not getting in trouble. I have no reason
to tell the truth because even when I do,
they don't praise me for my honesty."**

**"I lie because they don't trust me and I need
to be with my friends so I need to lie."**

I don't want to lay the whole burden of teens' lying on the parents, but from the teens' perspective, the more we respond irrationally, the more it pushes them to continue to lie.

Let's look at some research about lying and teens.

- Ninety-one percent of parents lie routinely and 59 percent lie regularly to their kids.[5]

- Forty-five percent of born-again teens believe lying is sometimes necessary, compared to 71 percent of teens not born-again.[6]

- Ninety-two percent of born-again teens agreed and 90 percent of teens not born-again agreed that what is right for one person in a given situation might not be right for another person in a similar situation.[7]

- "When it comes to matters of morals and ethics, truth

means different things to different people. No one
can be absolutely positive that they know the truth,"
66 percent of born-again teens agreed, and 87 percent of those not born-again agreed.[8]

❧ "There is no such thing as absolute truth—two people could define truth in conflicting ways and both
could still be correct," 59 percent of born-again
teenagers said they agreed while 78 percent of
teenagers not born-again agreed.[9]

If lying is an issue or is becoming an issue in your home, you have
a bigger problem than you think. Perpetual lies are like cancer in a
relationship. The very essence of a lie is "I can't trust you with the
truth, so I will tell you what I think you
want to hear."

If lying is the problem, you have no
basis for a relationship. The very foundation of a relationship—trust and
respect—is null and void. Teach your
children from an early age the importance of truth, the nature of a lie, and
what integrity is all about. Don't
assume that your young person knows
it is wrong to lie, but help her to understand *why* it is wrong. Teaching children to be truthful in their *hearts* at a
very young age will permeate every
area of their lives.

Here are a few tips for imparting
principles regarding truth to your
young person:

Ask yourself: "How much do I lie?" Our society is
so bombarded with lies that you may be telling an untruth and

not even realize it. Are you exaggerating the truth, stretching the truth, or telling a "white lie"? Assess your own truthfulness to see what kind of example you are setting.

Teach your young person that lying is a character flaw. Lying is the very nature of Satan himself. When we participate in lies it does something to our character. We become more like Satan. That is the harsh reality, but it is the truth.

Teach your teen about the nature of truth. James 5:12 says, ". . . Let your 'Yes' be yes, and your 'No,' no." Saying you will do something should be enough for someone to trust your word. Teach your young person the value of truth and truthfulness.

Teach your teen about integrity. Proverbs 11:3a says, "The integrity of the upright guides them." That means, if you are full of integrity and truthfulness, you are not always trying to keep up with your lies. If you walk with integrity, you walk securely.

Instill in your young person an understanding of "Whatever you do, don't ever lie to me." Your teen needs to know that whatever has transpired, you are the first person she comes running to. Carry yourself in a way that says, "No matter what you have done, no matter how bad it is, it is worse to lie." Your teen needs to feel a freedom to come to you in every situation. It doesn't mean she is granted immunity if she tells you the truth. It means that the consequences of lying are so much more severe that it makes her not want to lie.

Take time to ask questions, to listen, to make a relationship with her valuable, and you will "get through" on a daily basis and find that your influence is an important part of your teen's life.

FAMILY

Teach her the value of truthfulness so she will not try to live a secret life. Find ways of rewarding and blessing her for telling the truth in small and big matters. Building this kind of open, truthful environment into your home and your relationship puts you on the road toward a great, wholesome relationship with your young person.

If you suspect your teen is lying, don't constantly accuse her of lying. If you have caught her in an occasional lie, don't assume *everything* is a lie.

If you think your teen is lying and sneaking around, what you need to do is get enough facts to back up what you think. Then still don't say the "L" word, but sit your young person down when you have enough facts. Say something like this, "Mandy, remember how I've taught you the value of telling the truth? Remember how I've told you that no matter what you've done, you can come to me and tell me the truth? Now if you were to be completely truthful about this situation, is there anything else you would want to tell me?"

Instead of accusing her of lying, give her a chance to come clean and to empty her heart. It is good for her soul and heart. It is better for forgiveness and for your relationship. "At this moment, what matters is that you are being truthful. Is there anything else you want to say?" Then wait in silence for her response.

You then have a choice. You can say, "Okay, I trust you and believe you," if you don't have any *evidence* to the opposite. If you do, you might show her a bit of that evidence, but not all of it. What you're doing is showing her you know a little bit more than she thought you knew. So now she doesn't know how much you do know. That might help her be honest.

Keep giving her chances to come clean. "Why did you feel like you had to lie to me?" Give her consequences for lying, but more importantly, talk through it. Don't just talk about the thing she did, but talk about the lying as well. You need to have a trustworthy relationship, one in which you can count on the fact that your young person always tells you the truth. Make a big point about the lying issue, teaching her the importance of truthfulness, integrity, and being completely above board.

Young people do not learn about truthfulness and integrity by talking about it one time. Start when they are young—or now, wherever they are—and begin to share from the Scriptures the importance and value of living a life of total integrity without any lies.

talk to me, PLEASE

We want to hear about our teen's day and experiences, but when we ask questions about our teen's life, all we get is "I don't know."

What your teen is really saying in his "I don't know" response is that he doesn't know if he wants to tell you, rather than he doesn't know the answer.

> "I say 'I don't know' every time my parents
> try to start a conversation with me. They ask
> me what is wrong and I don't want to tell them
> because I don't want to hurt them."

> "Sometimes I don't even feel like I want to discuss
> stuff because I don't want to get in a fight.
> Sometimes it's just better not to bring it up."

In a study of teenagers, most identified several points they regard as important when their parents talk with them.

❖ Tell us you love us even if we act like we don't want to hear it.

❖ If we have a major problem, help us solve it. Don't solve it for us. If you do, we'll never learn how to function as adults.

❖ Never stop talking to us. You're the only ones we can count on for reassurance and love.[10]

Here are several ways to help your teen open up:

Talk about other interests, such as sports, movies, or music. Develop a relationship rather than demanding answers to some big important question. Your young person will do anything to protect his emotions and feelings from being slammed. He is a normal human being who wants to know that someone cares about *him*—not just his problems or one area of his life. Have great patience in developing a warm enough relationship so that when you ask a question, you will be less likely to hear, "I don't know."

Listen to conversations he brings up. Listen to what he talks about and use that to lead you into a deeper conversation. If he is talking about a certain event that just happened, don't change the subject. Ask simple questions to show you are interested. By asking heart-oriented questions about whatever he is talking about—whether it is friends, music, school, or a new movie—you will work your way into his heart. Always have your ear tuned in to statements that come from his heart. When he senses you care, you are going to hear the response "I don't know" less and less.

> "If I would say anything other than,
> 'I don't know,' it would turn into a big
> argument with my mom. I wish she would
> just understand me and not bother me."

Be careful how you respond to both the good and bad news your teen brings to you. Has he ever experienced a great victory, and as he excitedly tells you, you say, "Oh that's great," as you continue to read the paper? Or has he brought home some really heartbreaking news that may not sound upsetting to you but may have been devastating for him? Deciding to control your attitude and your words is a big step in getting through the "I don't knows." Take a deep breath and control your heart, mind, and emotions on a daily basis with your teen. As a result, when you ask the important questions, he'll be more likely to be straightforward and honest.

If your teen answers a question with, "I don't know," ask him, "What would you say if you did know?" Be careful to ask this without taking on a sarcastic or condescending attitude. It causes him to rethink the issue. The fact is he does know. Sometimes he is simply not in touch with how he feels or what he thinks. You would be amazed at how often he will actually come back with a response if you use a simple little conversation starter.

Getting through to your teen is most importantly linked to having a strong relationship with him. Take time to ask questions, to listen, to make a relationship with him valuable, and you will "get through" on a daily basis and find that your influence is an important part of your teen's life.

Parenting: Being an Effective Dad

chapter 2

loving your daughter

In *Parenting Isn't for Cowards*, Dr. James Dobson writes:

> "Most psychologists believe, and I am one of them, that all future romantic relationships to occur in a girl's life will be influenced positively or negatively by the way she perceives and interacts with her dad. If he is an alcoholic and a bum, she will spend her life trying to replace him in her heart. If he is warm and nurturing, she will look for a lover to equal him. If he thinks she is beautiful, worthy, and feminine, she will be inclined to see herself that way. But if he rejects her as unattractive and uninteresting, she is likely to carry self-esteem problems into her adult years." [1]

He will turn the hearts of the fathers to their children, and the hearts of the children to their fathers.
—Malachi 4:6

Your daughter may or may not be struggling with low self-esteem, but fathers need to make sure they are doing the things that will endear their daughters to them. Here are several ways you can do that:

Pray for your daughter. Ask God to turn your heart toward her, to help you love her with godly love, and to see her as God sees her. Spending time together and doing things with her are great, but make sure it is a result of your heart genuinely being drawn toward her through prayer.

Continue to pray for her. Think about what she is going through at school and with friends, and pray for those specific areas. Listen to stories and things that are going on in her life, and pray until your heart is overflowing with supernatural love from the Father. It will take a consistent commitment to praying for her.

Think of yourself as her spiritual father. How have you helped her grow in the Lord? Have you encouraged her in her walk with God? As you pray for her and let God woo your heart toward her, ask the Lord what to say to her. "Lord, what would You want me to share with her? What Scriptures would encourage her? How can she mature in her character and her walk with You?"

She needs to know that you are helping her grow spiritually. She needs to know she can come to you for advice, counsel, and encouragement because you hear the voice of God. Constantly pour into your daughter spiritually. She'll enjoy being around you because she'll feel like she is growing. You are blessing her, encouraging her, and helping her to take the next step in the Lord.

Is there anything you have said or done in the past that has

If girls don't get healthy affection or approval in a godly, fatherly way from their dads, they are going to look for it in the wrong way.

FAMILY

hurt her? It's amazing how one comment from a father can totally destroy his relationship with his daughter. Were you an absent father much of her childhood? Have you made comments about her looks or her weight? Until these things are dealt with, they can keep a distance between you.

Your relationship with your daughter will directly mirror her perception of what God the Father is like. Daughters who have been abused, put down, discouraged, or disillusioned by their physical fathers often reflect that kind of perspective toward their spiritual Father. Our responsibility is to represent the heart of God the Father. If we are successful in representing the kind of father He truly is, she will have the desire to know her Father in heaven.

Show your daughter the appropriate amount of male affection. Gordon McDonald writes:

Photo © Stockbyte

> Because a father is the first man to whom a daughter relates, that relationship is incredibly important—more so than most men realize. Daughters need to know that their fathers accept them as women and not just as little girls. . . . Daughters also need physical affection from their fathers. Some fathers feel embarrassed about giving attention to their daughters. They may have to push themselves and deliberately demonstrate affection until it becomes natural.[2]

Most fathers operate on one extreme or the other in the affection department. There is a balance in the middle where your daughter needs to know the wholesome affection of her father. That is, kissing her on the cheek, hugging her tight around the neck, and putting your arm around her when you're watching a television program together.

Dobson describes a daughter's need for appropriate affection:

> With girls, physical contact (especially the affectionate type) increases in importance as she becomes older and reaches a zenith at around the age of 11. What a critical time! . . . A child growing up in a home where parents use eye and physical contact will be comfortable with herself and other people. They will have an easy time communicating with others, and consequently be well-liked and have good self-esteem. Appropriate and frequent eye and physical contact are two of the most precious gifts we can give our children. . . . A father helps his daughter approve of herself by showing her that he approves of her. He does this by...unconditional love, eye contact, and physical contact, as well as focused attention. A daughter's need for her father to do this begins as early as two years of age. This need, although important at younger ages, becomes greater as the girl grows older and approaches that magic age of 13. One problem in our society is that as a girl grows older, a father usually feels increasingly uncomfortable about giving his daughter the affection she needs. This is extremely unfortunate. Yes, fathers, we must ignore our discomfort and give our daughters what is vital to them for their entire lives.[3]

God made male and female affection, fatherly and motherly affection in our lives to bring wholesomeness to children. If girls don't get healthy affection or approval in a godly, fatherly way from their dads, they are going to look for it in the wrong way. Hence, so many young ladies become promiscuous and advertise their bodies to get attention from males. What they are really looking for is wholesome male affection from their dad. If they get plenty of that, they won't need to look for affection from a guy, a date, or an

In our "machoism" we have passed on a legacy of cold-hearted relationships and missed the very richness of a heart-to-heart connection with our sons.

unwholesome romantic relationship. If some guy starts getting sweet on your daughter, giving her all kinds of compliments and accolades on how cute she is, the first thing that should pop in her mind is that her dad tells her that all the time.

Her heart should not be overwhelmed with a guy's sweet words to her. Her father gives her wholesome affection, says those kinds of things to her, and makes her feel valuable all the time, so she isn't star struck when a guy pays attention to her. In addition, she learns to recognize unwholesome, ungodly affection or attention, and it becomes a disdain, a disgrace, and a put-down to her— not something she longs for.

When we treat our daughters with respect, valuing them as precious before God, unashamed to hug them and kiss them on the cheek, to tell them we love them, and to shower them with compliments, we are putting protective measures in their lives.

loving your son

David Blankenhorn, chairman of National Fatherhood Initiative and president of the Institute for American Values, refers to father-lessness as "The most urgent domestic challenge facing the United States."[4] Kids without fathers are more likely to:

- ❖ Drop out of high school

- ❖ Abuse drugs

❧ Be in trouble with the law

❧ Be a victim of physical or sexual abuse

❧ Face emotional problems[5]

In 1960, 17.5 percent of teens lived apart from their biological fathers. By 1990, that percentage had doubled to 36 percent.

The tripling of teen suicides since the mid-1950s, the rise in chemical abuse, and the decline in SAT scores by 75 points between 1960 and 1990 are all trends that social scientists say were impacted by the absence of fathers.[6]

What is it about us fathers that make it tough to get close to our sons? Society's expectations for us to be macho, cool, hip, and not to cry or be emotional takes an amazing toll on our sons. In our "machoism" we have passed on a legacy of cold-hearted relationships and missed the very richness of a heart-to-heart connection with our sons.

"Real" men don't cry. Although it is true that camaraderie is built differently for guys than for girls, there sure are a lot of guys who grunt together but have never really even gotten to know each other on a friendship level, not to mention a father-son level. Society's idea of what a real man is—this elite, "macho" personality in shining armor—has to be seen for what it really is. We need to see how much we have let that mentality influence us, whether we realized it or not.

Maybe that is the way you were treated by your dad as you grew up. Dads have been acting this way for years. Very few sons have grown up with a wholesome relationship with their fathers, where they feel they can share anything and see their dad as their best friend.

If your dad treated you coldly, didn't have time for you, didn't connect with you heart-to-heart, or never really cried, laughed, or

If you want your son to grow to be a real man, you need to be the example of a real man—a spiritual father teaching him principles on which to build his life.

prayed with you, then it is only natural you have passed on that kind of relationship to your own son. Most of us learn our parenting skills from our own parents. Just because we were raised this way does not mean it is how we raise our own children. It's time for us to change the course. It's time to develop a wholesome relationship with our own sons.

Many of the principles for developing closeness with your son are the same as developing a relationship with your daughter. Begin to pray for him. Claim Malachi 4:6, "He will turn the hearts of the fathers to their children, and the hearts of the children to their fathers . . . ."

God will draw your heart close to your son. Don't just go through the motions of trying to be close, but really, genuinely care about what is going on in his life. Earnestly pray for him to be a man of God. Ask God to give him an incredible dream to make a difference in this world. Pray for God to be his confidence and the basis for his self-esteem, rather than feel the need to try to be "macho" according to the world's standard.

Are you being a true spiritual father to your son? Teach him what it takes to be a man of God. Show him Scriptures

Photo © Stockbyte

on being a real man with character and integrity like Christ. Does your son look up to you spiritually? If you want your son to grow to be a real man, you need to be the example of a real man—a spiritual father teaching him principles on which to build his life.

Remember, you are an example of God the Father. What your son sees in you is what he will think God is like. You can create an incredible legacy now by representing God in an accurate way and passing down an example that he in turn will live for his children, and they their children.

Is there anything you have done to push him away from you, whether purposely or inadvertently? Many fathers make the mistake of demanding so much from their sons; they can never live up to their fathers' expectations. He never feels approval or acceptance from his dad. He carries this around with him like a black cloud his whole life.

Many fathers have committed a sin of omission. They have not shared their heart or taken a chance to get close. *It's about being yourself.* It's about sharing who you are. It means taking time to sit down and talk with him.

What is your son really thinking and feeling? If you haven't asked and listened over the years, you have no doubt created an air of anger, resentment, and coldness. Your son has wanted someone he can share his heart with and talk with. These are just a few things that may have built a wall between you and your son. Blast through that wall by asking your son to forgive you. Be humble about it. Turn over a new leaf. Go against the grain of what

Remember, you are an example of God the Father. What your son sees in you is what he will think God is like.

society says a real man is. This will be the starting point of an incredible relationship between you and your son.

When God created the family with both a mother and a father, He knew it would take guidance, attention, input, and affection from both a male and a female for a young person to grow in a wholesome environment. The problem is that most of us men have never been shown wholesome affection. But we are not only emotional and spiritual beings—we are physical beings. And physical affection between a father and son is wholesome. Start putting your arm around his shoulders and letting him know he's important to you.

"As a boy grows and becomes older, his need for physical affection such as hugging and kissing lessens, but his need for physical contact does not. Instead of baby 'love stuff,' he needs 'boy-style' physical contact, such as bear hugs, 'give-me-five' hand slaps, and old-fashioned roughhousing." [7]

"Not all touches need to be physical to be effective," says William Beausay II, in his book *Boys! Shaping Ordinary Boys into Extraordinary Men.* Beausay says a dad can touch his son by:

- ❖ Asking his opinion

- ❖ Repeating his exact words after him

- ❖ Putting up a "welcome home" banner on the house after school

- ❖ Saying a poem with his name in it

- ❖ Splitting a bag of candy with him right before dinner

- ❖ Dropping everything and listening to him[8]

Tell him you love him. Don't assume he knows it. Tell him! It doesn't matter if he's 17 years old, give his shoulders a squeeze when he does something great. Put your arm around him when he is going through a struggle. All too often, young men who don't get proper affection from their fathers look for approval or affection from another male and end up in a homosexual lifestyle. When young men don't get the wholesome kind of affection, they turn to the unwholesome affection because it satisfies their longing for attention.

Get over this idea that says you're not a real man if you hug your son. Tell him you love him. It's time to be real. It's time to be honest. Take off the mask, look your son in the eye, and say, "I love you, son."

chapter 3
Fun: Enjoying Time Together

Are you starting to get a complex? Does it seem like every time you think you are going to have a little time to spend with your teenager she has something more important to do?

> "I am gone a lot because my mom always has something to do. I wish she'd actually try to make time for me, then I might stay home more often."

> "Whenever I am at home, I feel like I am walking on eggshells. I feel like no matter what I say, I am going to start an argument."

> "I wish my dad would stay home more often. He leaves at 4:45 a.m. and gets home about 7:00 p.m. I get so bored at home, and this is why I am always gone."

> "If my parents would back off more and let me stay closed up in my room by myself, I would stay home more often."

"I wish my parents would ask me to do
more things as a family instead of staying
home alone all of the time."

What is a parent to do?

First of all, understand you are not alone. This is a normal part of growing up. Psychologists have identified that in the first phase of life, a child's primary relationships are with parents. Children care about what their parents think and what they do.

Then there comes a point during adolescence when the primary relationship shifts from parents to friends as they learn to interact socially. This is healthy, because for the rest of your teen's life you want her to interact socially in a healthy way. Her decision to spend time with friends doesn't mean you are a bad parent or that there is something inherently wrong or bad about you. She is simply growing up.

where have you been?

How busy have you been throughout your teen's life—even when she was a child? Were you busy with work and activities? Maybe now things have slowed down for you, so you expect your teen to drop everything to be with you.

There could be hurt and resentment because you did not spend time with her when she was younger. If this is the case, it will take time to rebuild the relationship and show her you are truly sorry. It will take a while for her to realize you want to spend time getting to know her.

Make your home a place
filled with positive attitudes and
warmth—these qualities will
make your home a greenhouse.

Your home needs to be a green-house for your teen. Some young people have every high-tech toy you could imagine but don't want to be home. They feel like they're always walking on eggshells—someone is going to get mad and blow up. Who wants to be around that? Instead, make your home a place filled with positive atti-tudes and warmth—these qualities will make your home a greenhouse.

Photo © Big Cheese Photo

You may have to search your own heart and deal with atti-tudes in your own life. Create an atmosphere where your teen feels welcome, like she has arrived in a haven. She is in a place where she knows she is safe and protected from the world.

Your teen needs to feel wanted. Let her know you look forward to her being there. Cook her favorite food. Do you respect her opin-ion enough that you take her advice on things, such as painting a room a color she chooses? Make your home a refuge from the harsh realities of this world.

Don't demand that your teen stay home during her free time just for the sake of being there. If she is there physically but not emotionally, is it going to do much good? Include exciting events for her on your calendar of social activities.

Make your home the place young people in your community want to hang out when they come over to see your teen. Don't just say, "Stay home." Instead say, "Hey! Why don't you invite some friends over? You can rent a movie, buy some snacks and drinks, and I'll foot the bill."

Plan fun activities to do as a family and with friends—some-thing your teen could not do on her own with friends, because it costs too much money or she doesn't have the resources to do it. You are not trying to buy her love! You are trying to show her you care enough to provide fun in the context of your home. Home should not only be a place where she eats and sleeps, but also a place where she has fun with her family and friends.

Give her a legacy to look back on. In the end, your teen will remember the fond memories and times around the house with her friends—and you were the champion. You helped to shape her in your greenhouse—not to mention keeping her off the streets, away from the wrong parties, and out of compromising situations where trouble could have accidentally sprouted up.

chapter 4 Divorce: Sharing Your Teen with Your Ex

If you have been through the battle of divorce, you know the hurt and pain of separation from your former spouse and from your teen. Now that your young person is a teenager, he needs you the most for guidance and counsel.

Teens feel the effects of divorce:

> "I wish that when my mom talked to me she would say 'dad' like she used to when they were together. Instead she says, 'your dad' which makes it seems like she has nothing to do with him."

> "When my parents got divorced they never explained to me why. I'm in the custody of my mom and now my dad is giving me guilt trips about not staying at his house more often. I wish he would understand that I just like staying with my mom better."

> "My mom talked bad about my dad through the divorce. They treated each other with no respect around their children."

"They yelled about the other parent when
they were just as much to blame and made
me choose who to live with."

"I moved in with my dad because I fought
with my mom. I wish they would have learned
to communicate with each other better
and therefore prevented this."

The Center of Disease Control reports that the U.S. divorce rate for 2004 is around 50 percent. Divorce has taken its toll on the young people of this generation.[1] Josh McDowell lists the effects of divorce as denial, shame/embarrassment, blame/guilt, anger, fear, relief, insecurity/low self-esteem, grief, depression, alienation and loneliness, academic problems, behavioral problems, sexual activity, substance abuse, and suicide threats and attempts.[2]

Maybe you have partial custody of your teenager—part of the time he is with you and part of the time he is with your former spouse. Maybe you see him on weekends, every other week, or every six months. You can see that no matter how many letters you write or how many phone calls you make, it doesn't seem to do much good, so you are tempted to just cut everything off.

Sometimes, as a result of the divorce, we make it difficult for our teen to respect and honor the other parent through things we say, comments we make, or stories we tell.

honoring our ex-spouses

The best situation for your teen is to honor his parents (Eph. 6:2-3). The problem is that we get jealous. We don't want our teen to honor and respect the other parent more than us, so we tear the other one down, thinking he will like us more. We see our own interests as more important than the interests of our young person.

Help your teen to honor his other parent by not telling stories

Making the best out of a terrible situation helps teens respect both parents.

of hurt or everything your spouse did or said. You need to protect your ex-spouse and make him look good even when he may not deserve it. Why? Because you are protecting your teen.

Like it or not, your ex-spouse is still the parent of your child. When divorced persons play the childish game of being jealous for the attention and respect of their young person, it ends up harming the young person, ripping his heart and allegiance apart. Sometimes he believes you, sometimes he believes your ex-spouse.

That is one reason God hates divorce. (See Malachi 2:16.) He knows it rips apart the hearts of those getting divorced as well as the hearts of the children. Making the best out of a terrible situation helps teens respect both parents.

If you have said or done anything to run down your ex-spouse, as I'm sure most divorced persons have done from time to time (I know my parents did it all the time), ask your young person to forgive you. "I'm sorry for what I said about your dad. Even though I may not like him and we had our own reasons for divorce, I had no right to drag down your estimation of him."

This takes humility. In the long run, your young person will look back and see that you did not try to tear his heart away from the other parent. That says you are mature, secure, and not intimidated by someone else's success or respect.

Talk to your ex-spouse about agreeing on issues for the sake of your children. For example, agree on how you refer to each other and how you talk about each other. Don't ask him or her to constantly give you honor, but say, "Listen, I've decided that whenever I refer to you to our son or daughter, I am only going to say good things. We have had our differences and we made mistakes, but that is all behind us. We may not like each other, but you are still my son's mother or father, and I am going to afford you the respect you deserve because you hold that position."

That could be the starting point of the most wholesome kind of parenting that can take place between divorced parents. Then see if your ex-spouse will reciprocate. He may want to see if you are serious about it before deciding to do it himself. Don't let that inhibit you from doing what is right.

Agree on the rules you establish for your young person. So much dissension happens between a teen and his parents because, "Mom always lets me do this," and "Dad always lets me do that." The parents compete with each other to see how much fun they can let the teen have when he is at their house, hoping he will like them more and want to be with them more. The competition becomes a political game between the ex-spouses, and the best interest of the young person is not considered at all.

Talk through what is permitted and what is not, what kind of movies your teen can watch, and how late he can stay out. Commit to find some sort of middle ground on those areas you disagree on for the sake of your young person. It is not important—or even about—whom he likes the most. He will be healthiest if there is consistency between the two of you.

Agree about gifts—how much money you will spend on gifts and what each of you will get your teen for Christmas, birthdays, or other special holidays. If it is possible to have any kind of agreement on this, it will be much easier for the young person.

What do they really need? How much is too much? How much will

Photo © Big Cheese Photo

make him materialistic, self-centered, and feel like he always gets whatever he wants? Agree that you won't compete with each other, but that you will look beyond your own desires and needs to the needs of your teen.

Any time a teen visits one of his parents, he should not be showered with gifts the other spouse cannot afford. In such case, it would be noble for the parent who can afford it to give money to the parent who cannot afford it so there is equal exchange of gifts. Then the son doesn't grow up thinking one parent is better than the other because he gives him more "stuff."

Another challenge you might face is your teen's playing one parent against the other. "Mom lets me do it," or "Dad lets me do it." Comments like that will encourage competitiveness. But if you are on the same wavelength and in agreement on these issues, it will be almost impossible for your teen to manipulate you into that kind of situation.

If you do hear those remarks, stop them by saying, "We'll talk about it later." Then make a phone call to your ex-spouse. "Hey, is this something we haven't talked about that we need to come into agreement on?" If your teen knows he can't play you against one another, the competition will be defused rather than fueled. If your teen senses he can fuel it, he will.

including stepparents

In his book *Counseling Families After Divorce*, David R. Miller says, "Although parents see remarriage as a positive move, children often don't. They especially experience the fact that stepfamilies are born of loss. Studies show that being in a stepfamily is a risk factor for problems from dropping out of school to child abuse. Stepchildren are twice as likely to have behavioral problems as kids in nuclear families."[3]

If a stepparent is involved, the rules should always be enforced by the biological parent, not the stepparent. You never want the young person to respond to correction with, "Well, you're not my real parent anyway."

Sometimes a stepfather is called upon to enforce the rules because he is the man of the house. Although that is true, there is still a role that a biological parent has that a stepparent doesn't. The stepparent needs to earn the role, respect, and right. He doesn't get it simply because of marriage.

As a result of working with your ex-spouse, your teen will have a much better relationship with you and your ex-spouse, you will have at least a marginally pleasant and agreeable relationship with your former spouse, and your young person will be better for it.

friendships/relationships

All human beings want to belong. But teens, as they try to find out who they are, sometimes desperately seek this place to belong. Sometimes this search can lead them into situations with peer groups that you, as parent, may not approve of.

Belonging may be attached to friends or to a dating situation, but it is one that you, as a parent need to address. *What is your teen looking for? Who are his peers? How is he relating to the opposite sex?* In these cases, *is he looking for the right people for the right reasons?*

This search is what we hope to help you discern in your teen's friendships and dating relationships. As you provide the environment and home where your young person grows to feel accepted and loved, his search for belonging won't have to go far.

chapter 5 Friends: Needing to Belong

Peer pressure affects not only teenagers but also adults. Someone gets a nice car, so his neighbor has to get a nicer one. How many adults always want a better job, more pay, a bigger house, a bigger ring, or nicer clothes? Although it is obvious, we tend not to mention or notice it among adults, but we make it a huge issue among teenagers.

Researchers have found that teenagers pick friends with a similar age, gender, sexual experience, and academic and cultural orientation. Most teenagers place great importance on their friendships. About 62 percent of high school seniors surveyed say it's extremely important to have strong friendships. Teenagers spend more time with their friends each day than they do with their father, mother, both parents, or other adults—four hours with friends as compared to one hour with both parents.[1]

Nine out of ten teenagers say they experience peer pressure, and fewer than half of them say they try to stop peer pressure. The *TeenAge Magazine* reader survey also found that 80 percent of young people give in to peer pressure at least once a week, and 60 percent admit they pressure others.[2]

Teens listen to their peers most. So the question is, whom does

If you want your teen to be wise, get her around wise young people.

your young person choose to be around? Many parents feel totally helpless, as though they have no influence over their teenager's friends. This is simply not the truth.

who are your teen's friends?

Most young people have two sets of friends—their *church* friends and their *real* friends at school. Most of the time they don't want to be seen with their church friends when they are around their school friends. Their church friends are not really friends at all—they are acquaintances. They hang around them every week because their parents drag them to church, but they are not people they would choose to be around.

Parents pass it off with, "Well, it doesn't matter who my teen hangs out with most, as long as they are *good kids*." The problem is *good kids* can get into big trouble. The power of friendships and peer pressure among teenagers is something most parents don't remember and do not identify with. We hear about peer pressure, but we don't understand much of the tangled web of relationships it weaves.

And we have low expectations for the influence and control we as parents have. We think, "I have no control over who my teen meets at school." On the contrary, you *do* have control over where she goes to school, what kind of school she goes to, what extracurricular activities she does and with whom, and most importantly, what church and youth group she attends.

He who walks with the wise grows wise, but a companion
of fools suffers harm.
—*Proverbs 13:20*

If you want your teen to be wise, get her around wise young people. If you let her hang around fools, she will end up suffering harm, and her life will be the worse for it.

If your teen is not a Christian, or is a carnal Christian, ultimately she will do some very foolish things because she has no reason not to. Psalm 53:1 says, "The fool says in his heart, 'There is no God.'" With no moral strength, she has nothing guiding her greater than herself.

As parents we must influence our teens to be around young people who know how to use their free time wisely, how to spend money wisely, and how to develop wise friendships.

try church

Church youth groups can be helpful. "Since peers exert so much influence, a group of 'good kids' could push our teens in the right direction. This is where the church youth group and other Christian youth organizations come into the picture. They can provide Christian friends, a wholesome atmosphere, and solid content."[3]

Charles R. Swindoll shares a story about his children:

We tried to get them to think about the type of people they wanted to spend their time with—people who would strengthen them morally, people

It is possible to build an open, *influential* relationship by doing things together, talking, listening, and accepting her as an emerging adult.

with good self-esteem. We stressed the advantage of finding friends with good parents and homes with high ideals. I remember when one of our daughters chose a friend who wasn't good for her. She's a sensitive girl and was easily swayed in her early years. We sat her down one day and just talked about her friend—what her home life was like, and what the characteristics of her family seemed to be. Then we asked our daughter what things she liked in our home and what was important to her.

I asked her to think about the parallels between her life and the life she wanted, and that of her new friend. As I suspected, she couldn't think of too many. By realizing that there was such a marked contrast between her life and ideals and those of her new friend, my daughter began to see things in a new light.[4]

Some key concepts to consider:

Relationship. Become a "peer" in your young person's life. It is possible to build an open, *influential* relationship by doing things together, talking, listening, and accepting her as an emerging adult.

Dialogue. To steer your teen toward the right kind of friends, you must open channels of communication. Show genuine interest in her and her activities and spend time talking.

Open home. Let your teen know your home is open for her friends. Instead of condemning her peers and pointing out faults, invite them to dinner or some other social opportunity.

You may hear comments from your young person like, "All the Christians I meet are weird. I can trust my non-Christian friends more than I can my Christian friends." And that is probably true. Adults could say the same thing. Yet in spite of all that, there *are* young people who passionately love God with all their hearts. Those are the ones you need to get your teen around. The question is *how*.

- ❖ Diligently search until you find an incredible youth group or youth ministry for your young person.

- ❖ Take your young person to every kind of Christian youth activity you can find.

Do not choose a church simply based on whether *you* like the Sunday morning service. This is a matter of life or death for your teen because of the strong influence that peers have in teenagers' lives.

Some parents find something their teen really likes and then begin to revoke it as a punishment if she does something wrong. Parents must realize that they cut off the *spiritual growth* of their

Right now is the time, in the formulating stages of your teen's life, for her to stay around as many on-fire young people as she possibly can.

young person when they take away the privilege of participating in church and youth group. There are plenty of ways to correct without taking away the things of God.

Though it is a sacrifice to run our teens back and forth to church and different activities, we do it for sports, ballet, cheerleading, etc. Those things will pass away, but how she walks with God will direct the rest of her life.

Getting your teen around a group of young people to really develop friendships means letting her go to camp, conventions, retreats, and mission trips. It will help her walk with God and gain friends who really love God. Because peers are such a great influence, she will be constantly influenced to seek more of God.

For the sake of your young person, her walk with God, and her survival as a Christian, do whatever is necessary to make sure she is constantly around young people who have the fire of God. Exposing her to the right kind of friends will help her seek her need to belong in the places where the influence is positive.

Right now is the time, in the formulating stages of your teen's life, for her to stay around as many on-fire young people as she possibly can. Direct your teen to the places you would like her to belong and build relationships. Your son or daughter will be a teenager only once.

chapter 6
Dating: Finding the Right Date

Have you noticed a glow in your teen's eye? You don't know what could possibly be going on for him to be so full of energy and life these past few weeks. He tells you about this girl who has been noticing him lately, and now he has the courage to ask her out on a date. Never mind the fact that he is only 14 years old. What is a parent to do?

teens and dating

Some parents think they have no choice—their teen will pursue a romantic relationship anyway, so why fight it? They feel like they have to say yes, and as a result, open the door to a whole new set of arguments, frustrations, and confusions. They assume this is just a normal stage in the development of a teenager's life. The issue is not whether you say "yes" or "no" about your teen's going on this date. The issue is bigger than that.

What have you taught your young person about dating before this point? Has he learned it from those who are least qualified to teach the right way to pursue godly love, dating, or a relationship? Have you taught him to *pray* about dating someone? The cute girl or the cool guy your teen is interested in may be sending all the right signals, but unless you and your teen have a peace from God, the relationship should go no further than a friendship.

Our culture has bombarded teens with ways to pursue dating relationships. You don't have to look very far to see the results: broken hearts, immorality, and broken marriages. It is imperative that we teach our young people about relationships in general. This includes learning how to develop a friendship which can ultimately lead to a happy romance.

A desire for a date may be just the motivation needed to start a series of conversations to teach them how a godly relationship should develop. Instead of just saying "yes" or "no," begin by saying, "You know I wanted to talk to you about relationships anyway, and about some of the wise principles in developing the right kind of relationship. Let's talk about this."

Here are commonly held myths about teenage dating and principles to help diffuse them.

Myth #1: If I don't date, I won't be popular—I won't have any fun as a teenager and everyone will see me as totally weird.

Young people are raised with the notion that they must date. It is not a matter of *if*, it is a matter of *when* and *who*. There is no wisdom or forethought put into what kind of person they should go out with or how to properly begin a relationship.

Our culture has bombarded teens with ways to pursue dating relationships. You don't have to look very far to see the results: broken hearts, immorality, and broken marriages.

The average person falls in and out of love 10 times before he marries. Then he walks down the aisle, looks at his bride, and says, "Here is the one little leftover piece of my heart I saved for you."

The fact is, thousands of young people have fun every night of the week and don't have a boyfriend or girlfriend. They have wholesome friends who know how to laugh heartily, get wild, and be crazy without their hearts being attached to another person. In the long run, they will have much more fun with a group of friends than they would by being a part of the dating scene.

Myth #2: Falling in love is just a normal part of growing up. Everyone is bound to do it and get his heart broken.

The average person falls in and out of love 10 times before he marries. Think about that. What does that say? The average person falls in love, breaks up, gets his heart ripped out—No. 1. He falls in love again, breaks up, gets his heart ripped out—No. 2. He falls in love again and again until No. 10. His heart is literally broken 10 different times before finally finding the one to marry. Then he walks down the aisle, looks at his bride, and says, "Here is the one little leftover piece of my heart I saved for you."

I don't believe that is God's best or His plan for marriage! Song of Solomon 2:7 says, ". . . Do not arouse or awaken love until it so desires." That is repeated two more times in Song of Solomon 3:5 and 8:4. What does it mean? It is making reference to physical sex and the act of making love, but it also indicates opening the heart and allowing it to be ripped apart.

Until your young person is ready to develop a relationship that will last the rest of his life, no part of his heart and life is safe to

Photo © Comstock

open up to anyone. The problem is that most young people cannot distinguish which part of their heart is which. Proverbs 4:23 says, "Above all else, guard your heart, for it is the wellspring of life." We need to teach our teens to guard their hearts. We need to teach them the wise way to pursue a relationship.

Most parents grew up having fallen in and out of love, and we like the idea that it might be happening to our young person. "It is so sweet. It is so nice. You can see the sparkle in his eye." And then your young person loses his purity.

Many young people who have committed to purity end up getting involved sexually—not because they meant to, but because they gave their heart away. In fact, one study reports that 16.7 percent of teenagers who pledged to remain virgins until they are married ended up having sex before marriage (20.6 percent of girls and 11.2 percent of boys).[1] Many well-meaning people who gave their heart away first and then their body have lived with remorse for years after. They couldn't understand how it happened. *Giving your heart away to another person puts the other person in control of your life.* They can jerk the heart-string and make you do whatever they want.

Teach your teen to hold on to his heart. He can have acquaintances and have fun with people, but he shouldn't let his heart go. Warn your child not to open his heart before he is mature enough to know what to do with those feelings. If you teach him early in life, it will save him years of heartache and heartbreak. He should give his heart to Jesus and save the rest for the one he will spend the rest of his life with.

friendship leads to romance

Help your teen understand that a healthy *romance* must first start with a healthy *friendship*. A sparkle in someone's eye sitting across the room in geometry class is not an ingredient of a healthy friendship. At the end of a breakup, most young people—as well as older people—will say, "I would never have dated that person if I had really known him." But regarding people she has known for a long time, she says, "Oh! I know him way too well. We are too good of friends to date." She is contradicting herself and doesn't even know it!

Most people date because they want someone to share their heart with. They want a real friend. But most dating in America is so plastic and contrived that the very thing they want—a close friendship with someone—is the very thing they don't get.

She is trying to be what she thinks the other person wants,

Most dating in America is so plastic and contrived that the very thing they want—a close friendship with someone—is the very thing they don't get.

Teach your teen about courtship, which begins with a wholesome friendship when she is mature, wise, and strong enough to handle a romance.

and with both people doing that, no one ever really knows what the other person is really like. Once your teen asks you if she can go out on a date, begin a series of conversations that will help her understand the right way to pursue a relationship.

Help her understand she doesn't need to play the American dating game in which her heart gets broken many times before she gets married. Instead, teach your teen about courtship, which begins with a wholesome friendship when she is mature, wise, and strong enough to handle a romance. She should be accountable to parents, friends, and leaders so she doesn't accidentally slip up and give away her purity. Have her set guidelines for the kind of person she wants to date, the kind of person she wants to be before she dates, and how she wants to carry herself in a dating relationship—*before* she enters one.

You might say this is much too complicated for a teen—she just wants to go on a date. Not so! I have seen dozens of young people who have committed to courtship instead of dating and have been spared the brokenness of lost purity and lost trust. They have avoided the legacy of relationship mishaps that scar so many of our pasts.

This is not a hoax, a dream, or a fairy tale. This is reality— living life by principles found in the Word of God. It will rescue your young person from so much of what you as a parent have already been through.

You can't regulate your teen's heart. You can't tell her whom to love. But you can help her sort out what real love is. Many different forms of infatuation purport to be *love*, and we must help our teens sort through the confusion.

As you teach your teen the principles of real friendship, wholesome relationships, and godly romance, she will begin to take on her own values and develop relationships according to wisdom. We can help keep our teens from awakening their love before it is time.

chapter 7 Homosexuality: Avoiding the Trap

A 2005 movie, *Brokeback Mountain*, stars two of the hottest young actors, Heath Ledger and Jake Gyllenhaal, in a 1950s western. You're probably thinking cowboys riding the range, meeting beautiful women, but no, it is the story of two men who fall in love with each other, and through the years, fight their natural feelings for each other although they have married women and had children. Of course, these two stars will draw teens to the movie.

Whatever we do—reading the paper, watching television, going to the movies—we find the homosexual lifestyle as an accepted way of life. Homosexuality is becoming more commonplace in family hour sitcoms. There is a channel specifically for gay people. There are lead gay characters in many heterosexual sitcoms or very prominent lead roles for gay characters in big-screen dramas and comedies. How does this impact our children when they see that the homosexual lifestyle is an acceptable way to live?

First, ask yourself how much media your teen is exposed to. What is he watching on television? What magazines does he read? Gage the influence that culture may be having on your teen. How does he view the gay lifestyle?

Whatever we do—reading the paper, watching television, going to the movies— we find the homosexual lifestyle as an accepted way of life.

The June 2005 issue of *Seventeen* featured three articles: "How to Tell If You're a Lesbian," "How to Tell Your Parents If You Are a Lesbian," and "How to Have Safe Lesbian Sex."[1] Our kids see homosexuality everywhere through music, MTV, or TV commercials that show girls interacting with girls. The more your teens are exposed to this kind of stuff, the more they will believe the lie that says, "I was born this way"; "It's biological"; "It's normal, just a different lifestyle."

talk, talk, talk

Talk to your teen about homosexuality, not in a preachy way, but in a way that fosters honest discussions about what he sees in media. What are his attitudes and perspectives about homosexuality? Where is he getting his information?

The world says no one chooses whether or not he is gay. The goal is to "discover" who you are. I've met many young people who are trying to discover if they are gay or not, so they experiment with both genders sexually even while they are young. They want to see what feels most natural to them.

The Bible is clear about God's standards regarding homosexuality both in the Old and New Testaments. Romans 1:24 says, "Therefore God gave them over in the sinful desires of their hearts to sexual impurity for the degrading of their bodies with one another." In the story of Sodom and Gomorrah in Genesis 19, we see that God loves the person but does not agree with the lifestyle.

People may say, "I was born this way," but there is no biological proof of this. Some studies that scientists have used to prove that homosexuality is genetic could never be reproduced. Because we hear, "It's genetics," over and over, we start believing it whether it's true or not. We just think it's common knowledge.

Just because someone is interested or attracted to someone of the same sex does not mean he is homosexual. We are tempted with all kinds of sin. It's like reflecting any other sin; you resist, repent, and you need to put pure thoughts in your mind. Help your teen understand this process in his relationship with God.

Teenage girls and guys are tempted to experiment. While they may know that homosexual behavior can lead to sexually transmitted diseases in *other people*, they believe themselves to be invincible. And a little experimenting seems harmless. They do not understand that in experimenting, they, too, can get diseases like HIV, chlamydia, and syphilis.

What they are looking for is what "feels" more natural. If homosexual activity feels more natural than heterosexual, then they

FRIENDSHIPS/RELATIONSHIPS

Photo © Comstock

Help your teen discover the person *God* has made him to be. Help him get his identity from Christ and not our culture.

might think that's the way they are. Or if each feels the same, a teen might conclude he is bisexual. Like any other sin, if teens are attracted and tempted by it, they need to resist it.

If your teen is experimenting with homosexuality or asking questions, show him Christ's love. Find out what is going on in his life, listen first, and talk second. Rather than avoiding him because you disapprove of his choices, intentionally spend even more time with him.

Many young men and women get involved in homosexuality because of situations they experienced. Maybe a young man was abused as a boy or hurt by a father. Maybe a young woman was hurt by a male and finds herself drawn to women so that she isn't hurt again. Teens need help dealing with the deeper hurt and the core issue.

Some young men end up thinking they are gay. My contention is that no one is gay. He might think or believe he is. If a man says he is attracted to men and "I'm made that way," he is choosing to be attracted to a man.

Help your teen discover the person *God* has made him to be. Help him get his identity from Christ and not our culture.

"It's just the way it is these days, Mom and Dad . . ."

The entertainment media is the dominant form of influence on our young people today. The more they watch, the more they accept certain norms as the way the world is.

Only 35 percent of baby boomers firmly believe in Scripture, and thus have shaped our culture with the following results:

- Morally corrupt films and television programs
- An increasingly perverted music industry
- The pornographic invasion of the Internet
- Civil initiatives promoting gay marriages
- Battles to remove the Ten Commandments from public buildings, and fights to take "under God" out of our Pledge of Allegiance[1]

Without a doubt, our teens think that what they see on TV, the Internet, school, etc. shape what is acceptable today.

But parents need to hold firm to their family and its standards, no matter what your teen tells you is okay. Help protect your teen from the influences of our world today.

chapter 8 — Music: "I Don't Listen to the Words"

"I love rock music."

"I have no desire to quit listening to secular music. It affects me in no other way but emotionally."

"I listen to rock music and my parents like oldies. They are not Christian songs, but they consist of good music. I am intelligent and I do not believe that just because I don't listen to Christian music, I have a problem. I have no problem. I listen to music that I like, and I don't really have a liking for Christian music."

So many parents' attitudes are:

"I cannot stop them anyway. They are going to do what they want to do when they are not with me."

"I have listened to secular music my whole life, and I am not that bad of a person."

Musicians have been called
        "modern-day philosophers."
Musicians have the power to
        shape society and the thought
patterns of young people.

Music today influences so much of a teen's identity, drawing her into a whole subculture according to the music she listens to. *Music can make her feel she belongs.*

Some teens listen to it only occasionally. Others are obsessed, constantly having on their headphones, walking around in "another world," or watching MTV. Their philosophy of life and interactions with other people are dictated by their music.

Musicians have been called "modern-day philosophers." Musicians have the power to shape society and the thought patterns of young people.

music's impact

The impact of music and media on young people today is unprecedented. Quentin Schultze says, "In this type of adolescent culture, where identities are up for grabs and where adult-adolescent communication is weak, the media plays an unprecedented role in teenage life. First, the media challenges the authority of parents, pastors, and teachers. Teens look to media celebrities for styles of dress, acceptable behavior, and even values and beliefs to guide their lives. Rock-music stars, television characters, and radio personalities are mentors and teachers, not just entertainers."[1]

James Dobson says, "It is difficult to overestimate the negative impact music is having. Rock stars are heroes, the idols that young people want to emulate. And when they are depicted in violent and sexual roles, many teenagers and preadolescents are pulled along in their wake."[2]

Mike Shalett, founder of the music information system SoundScan, stated, "Every generation needs music that screams rebellion to parents. Alternative did that, but it was quickly co-opted. Now labels need to provide some kind of rebellious, anthemic music that the young consumer can call their own." A special subcommittee of the American Medical Association reports that the average teenager listens to 10,500 hours of rock music between the seventh and twelfth grades.[3]

What if your young person has been sucked into this?

Don't come right out and say, "We are never having that music again in our house!" Your teen may not listen to it in the house, but she may still be listening to it outside the home. Talk with her so she will want to put *her* foot down and not just stop listening to it because you say so.

What can you do to guide her through the process?

- ❧ Look at the song lyrics of her favorite music. Sit down together and look over them. If you do not understand some of the lyrics, ask your teen what they mean.

- ❧ Compare them to Scripture.

- ❧ Read magazine articles about the bands. Find interviews, and read them with your young person.

CULTURE

Teach her how to make a wise decision for herself, rather than just saying, "Don't listen to it because I say so."

❖ See what the band members are like. What have they
   done with their lives? What lifestyle do they lead?
   Are these people you want influencing your teen's
   life? Are they Christians? How long have they been
   Christians? Are they accountable to anyone?

Teach her how to make a wise decision for herself, rather than just
saying, "Don't listen to it because I say so." At the very least, show
your teen you are informed and interested, that your recommenda-
tion not to listen is for legitimate, logical reasons, not that you
simply don't like it.

Show your teen that you care enough about what they are
doing to be involved with them. Psalm 101:4 says, "Men of per-
verse heart shall be far from me; I will have nothing to do with
evil." Many young people say, "I just listen to the music. It won't
influence me because I don't listen to the words. They are just a
popular group." On the contrary, the lyrics *do* influence their minds
and the way they think, whether they believe it or not.

The spiritual implications of listening to secular music are
incredible. Many secular musicians do not have high standards or
ethics. Most of them drink and abuse
drugs. Often these bands, trying to be
creative, write music after getting
drunk or high on drugs. The group
comes up with lyrics, sings the song,
and puts it on a CD. Now your
good, church-going young person, who loves the Lord but
likes listening to secular
music, hears it. She
never had any desire
to do drugs, drink,
etc., but because they
are pumping this

You do have influence. You can set guidelines and parameters so your teen will be raised in a wholesome environment.

music into her brain, she is hearing someone who has been influenced by the demonic world. The music may be blatantly rebellious as they "sing about the devil," or it may have more subtle lyrics.

The spirit of the musician is infused into the spirit and the heart of the young person listening to that musician. Young people can get the same demonic oppression without being on drugs or alcohol because they are getting it directly from the person who created and produced these songs—inspired by the enemy of our souls.

"What about love songs?" your teen may ask. Love songs are not wrong if they are inspired by God's love. But if the songs are inspired by the world's viewpoint and the enemy's perspective, they'll have a skewed version of love. Young people listening to them will end up with confused ideas on love and what a wholesome relationship is all about.

For the sake of your young person and her spiritual and emotional survival, help her to understand the ramifications.

Finally, brothers, whatever is true, whatever is noble, whatever is right, whatever is pure, whatever is lovely, whatever is admirable—if anything is excellent or praiseworthy—think about such things.
—Philippians 4:8

Nothing is inherently wrong with a particular style of music, but what is more important is the spirit and attitude behind the musician singing or writing the music. Instrumental music has no words to convey the spirit and the heart of the musician, but no matter what style of music it is, if it is not written and performed by those with hearts and minds focused on the Father, it can take your teen down the wrong path.

Why in the world would anyone who wants to live with God in the center of her life want to be influenced by someone living a life without God? Help her see the lifestyles of the singers and bands. Show her they are singing about life from a perspective that is dark, depraved, and at the very least, without God.

You can limit how much time your teen spends listening to a CD or MP3 player by telling her you don't think it is wise for her to listen to music all day long. Suggest she listen to praise and worship or teaching CDs. You do have influence. You can set guidelines and parameters so your teen will be raised in a wholesome environment.

chapter 9 — Television: "Just One More Show"

Turn up the volume. Rent another movie. Watch another television program. Instead of relating to a person, your teen has a relationship with a video screen. He has a difficult time with any relationship. He doesn't know how to work things out and he often shuts things out. In addition, he is also receiving much of his philosophy of life through music, television, and movies.

We have such a media-craved, media-controlled society that it has diverted attention away from interaction and personal relationships. If people can't get along, can't work out a situation, or are just tired of being with people, it's easy to retreat to something they don't have to argue with, that won't talk back to them, something they can enjoy.

The question is, "How much is too much?" It's probably unrealistic to think your young person will actually shut the television off and never turn it back on. But where should parents draw the line? How can you draw the line in a way that is palatable to everyone and makes sense to your young person?

The typical American household has a television on seven hours a day. Teenagers watch approximately 21 hours of TV a week.[1] Watching television is cited as the favorite leisure activity among teenagers, with 80 percent of those surveyed saying they watch

CULTURE

television during their leisure time. Teenagers are the people with the most amount of leisure time at their discretion.[2]

About 50 percent of all teenagers have a television in their rooms.[3] Nearly 61 percent of all television programming contains violence, with children's programming being the most violent.[4] So much television-watching robs the family of opportunities for interaction.

I now know now my family is under attack by the king of lies. God has put on my heart that I must get active for the souls of my babies. Just this past Saturday I was shown how shocking and bad things have gotten for our children. I found my two young ones watching music videos . . . these videos are pornography . . . they were watching a girl wearing next to nothing being rolled around in paint by several males.

—*Parent of a Teen*

Bob Keeshan, of *Captain Kangaroo* fame, said, "Television is really part of the extended family now in people's homes. It's right in the living room. Ninety-nine percent of parents don't care what their children watch on television because the parents use it as a baby-sitter."[5] Even among teenagers, as long as we know they are not getting in trouble, we don't really care what they are doing. *We let television raise our young people and dictate their values.*

violence permeates television

Among the violent acts seen on television, 73 percent of the perpetrators go unpunished. Most violent portrayals do not show the consequences of a violent act—47 percent show no harm to victims, 58 percent depict no pain, and only 16 percent show long-term consequences. Twenty-five percent of violent television incidents involve the use of handguns which, according to a study, can "trigger aggressive thoughts and behaviors."[6] Christian teens are more likely to watch MTV (42 percent) than their non-Christian peers (33 percent). The typical teen will allocate roughly one quarter of their television attention—about 25 minutes a day—to MTV.[7]

"By graduation day, the average high school student has seen 18,000 murders in 22,000 hours of television viewing. According to studies done at the Annenburg School of Communications in Philadelphia, 55 percent of prime-time characters are involved in violent confrontations once a week."[8]

How does watching television affect families? It can disrupt communication among family members and negate socialization skills. Perspective is lost if kids are watching television shows alone with no parental input or discussion. As a result, kids are getting a distorted view of social reality. They view those 20,000 murders (before the age of 18) without parents helping them understand that murder is wrong.

Viewers consider television personalities, like news anchors or soap opera/sitcom actors, more like friends than people who are actually in their lives.[9] Even with all this television-watching and

CULTURE

Be aware of how much television your young person is watching, whether it is at a friend's house or in the living room of your own home.

Have we let the media become a surrogate parent?

the availability of television in their rooms, 75 percent of teenagers say that if given a choice between television and family time, they would opt for family time.[10]

Again, what is a parent to do? *Be aware of how much television your young person is watching, whether it is at a friend's house or in the living room of your own home.* Find out what is being fed into his heart and mind. Also be aware of what programs he is watching—not just their names, but what the shows are about. Remember, what your teen watches will instill values, shaping him for his present and future life. It will depress or inspire, motivate or discourage.

The bombardment of negative media is overwhelming to a parent. Most parents have a hard time saying "no"—let alone "no" to TV, Internet, etc. Often if you do, your kids go to a friend's house anyway. We have had no TV for four weeks now. (Movies are still allowed, although I would like to cut that back, too.) Internet is monitored. I have noticed a few things with our 14-year-old as a result. She is softer and more responsive to hugs and praise. She is more creative; she painted a picture one night; she plays the piano, writes songs, and, yes, even cleans her room. She used to watch *MTV, The Simpsons, Family Guy, That '70s Show,* etc. She has always been strongly influenced by media, from her clothes to her language and attitudes. Although I taught her much differently, she believes most of what is on TV and thinks her life should be like Paris Hilton's. We are no longer in a constant battle over the TV remote—it's great!

—*Parent of a Teen*

take control

Take control of the influences affecting your young person. Do this very diplomatically because up to this point she has had control. She could flip channels as much as she wanted, going through the cable and satellite channels at her own discretion. If all of a sudden you come down hard and say, "No more TV!" she may react negatively.

You are going to have to show her your desire for a better relationship. Let her know you desire to do more family activities together, to actually experience adventure rather than just watch it.

Is her leisure/extracurricular time being flushed down the drain by television, or are you designing character-building/relationship-building activities to enrich your family? Are you playing games together, *talking* at the dinner table, and taking day trips with your family, or does the tube do most of the talking in your home? When your young person reflects on her growing-up years, what will she remember doing most with her leisure time?

Decide what programs and/or movies you will watch together. Sit down as a family and talk about *why* certain situations portrayed are right or wrong. Use these opportunities to instill character and teach lessons, as opposed to just sitting in front of the television and vegging out.

Or why not unplug the television set? We unplugged ours and just watch videos instead. Yes, we can hook the television back up for special things like a ball game now and then, but we rarely do it. I trust my kids, but I don't trust that crazy Hollywood. (There are

CULTURE

a lot of benefits; it's amazing how many toys my kids *don't* ask for at Christmas anymore.)

Think of how much television you watch and how absorbed *you* get. *Monitor your own TV-watching habits.* Do you sit there and respond, "Yes, Dear," or "No, Dear," to your teen without really listening? Are you asking your young person to quit watching so much television, yet you are absorbed in it yourself?

Again, Psalm 101:3 says, "I will set before my eyes no vile thing . . . ." Don't let anything that is going to corrupt you, distract you, or pull you away from letting God enter your heart or mind.

Have we let the media become a surrogate parent? Do we wonder, "How could my teen actually think or act like that? Where did she get that attitude from?" when all the while we have let the television come into our living room and kidnap her heart and mind? Let's be the parents God wants us to be by actively helping to shape the perspective of our young people as they develop into young adults.

chapter 10 Internet: "They're Just Pictures"

You put the computer in his room as a tool for schoolwork. Internet access helps him do research for projects. Maybe you even set up some filters so that your teen could not access certain websites. But you have begun noticing that he is spending lots of time at the computer. Does he have that much homework? And there've been some nights that you have discovered him on the computer at 2 or 3 a.m. What could he be doing?

The Internet—it has revolutionized our world with the amount of information we have access to, the speed with which we can access it, and the kind of information we can find without leaving our home. But the Internet is another form of media that is reaching into our homes and into the hearts of our teens.

teens and the internet

The first generation of point-and-click Internet porn can now directly demonstrate to us the damage done to the soul and psyche of our teens. A limitless variety of porn lingers just a click away, ready to be delivered via high-speed cyber connections straight to the anonymous comfort of your computer chair.

This great new technology we all benefit from is also wreaking havoc on our kids. The odds of avoiding it seem hardly fair, because kids don't even have to deliberately go looking for the garbage: By 1999 "one in five children between the ages of 10 and 17 received a sexual solicitation over the Internet, and one in 33" were approached for a direct contact in some manner.[1]

Based on her Department of Justice study, Dr. Judith Reisman, president of the California Protective Parents Association, states that "much of the multi-billion dollar pornography industry focused on attracting 12- to 17-year-old boys to ensure lifetime addiction-consumers."[2] This juvenile marketing strategy is arguably similar to that employed by Big Tobacco, but the target market seems even younger. The average age of first Internet exposure to pornography is 11 years old.[3]

So, when teens receive an e-mail that throws them to a porn site, they're already baited and ready to become addicted. That's why Family Safe Media can report that 80 percent of 15- to 17-year-olds have had multiple hard-core porn exposures. And 90 percent of 8- to 16-year-olds have viewed porn online (most while doing homework).[4] For many parents, these statistics may not seem like cause for concern. After all, better your teen be looking at porn that actually having sex, right? But research shows that pornography is not as harmless as it may seem. In the 1970s, neurologists discovered that viewing pornography permanently changes the brain! Reisman says that every single time a person sees a pornographic image, his brain physiologically changes, bringing him closer to addiction.[5]

This great new technology
          we all benefit from is also
wreaking havoc on our kids.

What does this mean for your teen? It means that viewing pornography *now* will impact him negatively *for the rest of his life.* Pornography is static, impersonal, and unfeeling. When a teen views pornographic images, his sexual desires are awakened by something that cannot show affection, feel hurt, or experience emotion. What he knows of sex is void of human interaction, passive and completely *self*-fulfilling. As he grows in addiction, he moves further and further away from ever being able to experience God's design for marriage—His perfect plan for physical, emotional, and spiritual unity between husband and wife.

Pornography isn't just a little concern; it's a *huge* deal. How can you protect your teen from the influence of the Internet? "I will set before my eyes no vile thing," says Psalm 101:3. I would extend it like this: "I will let no vile thing come before the eyes of my family." We can frame all the family documents we want, but if the world is bombarding our kids at will every day, how can we fight back?

Photo © Photodisc

CULTURE

My 16-year-old daughter struggled BIG TIME with the Internet. She was solicited several times, often due to her checking out dating sites and setting up her own web page, hidden to us on a site we found through spyware on her computer. We found inappropriate pictures she had put on it, and she ran away several times to go meet someone. She lied, often didn't go to school this last year, cut herself, had sex, and got a sexual disease. She hated everything about her life. We intervened when she said she couldn't stand to live with us and our rules anymore and sent her to a boarding school. We feared that the next time she ran away with someone, she would never return home. She has been six months now at a very strict school. She turned to God and has totally turned her life around. Her relationship with the Lord is amazing! She now gets why we have the values we have. We went to see her a month ago to do a seminar together, and she, herself, felt she wasn't ready to come home yet. She feels that the Internet was her biggest downfall and biggest temptation. Her plan when she returns is to do up a contract with her friends and family about her commitment to not be on the Internet. She has also asked us to not have the Internet in our home.

—Parent of a Teen

safeguard your home

First, do an evaluation of your time with your teen. Are you spending quality time together so that he is not looking other places for family or community? God calls us to a relationship with Him as well as creating an atmosphere in our homes for our teens to have a relationship with God. If all we or they do is spend time with media, God is crowded out. You, as the parent, have control over your home.

Next, bring the computer out into a common area of your home. It is far more difficult to view inappropriate material if you know someone is "watching."

Establish rules for Internet use that include how much time your teen can spend on the Internet and monitor his e-mail, if possible. It doesn't mean you read the e-mail, but you can make sure there is nothing coming into your home that you don't recognize.

Put a filter on your Internet. Don't rely on software filters, because teens can often find ways to "hack" them. Instead, sign up with an Internet service provider that filters content at the server level. There are scores of such companies to choose from, but you might start your search with Web sites like these:

- www.afafilter.com

- www.hedge.org

- www.cnonline.net

- christianbroadband.com

When you relate to your teen in normal conversation, be careful not to shy away from the topic of pornography. Often, boys and girls begin viewing pornography out of youthful curiosity, but curiosity can quickly become addiction. It's vital that your teen not only understands that pornography is bad, but why it's bad. Model for your teen a holy horror toward pornography and a sincere, consistent respect for women.

CULTURE

Next, bring the computer out into a common area of your home. It is far more difficult to view inappropriate material if you know someone is "watching."

Make your home a safe haven for your teen. Do whatever is necessary to ensure that pornography and other influences are not finding a way into your home.

Finally, if you discover your teen is involved in pornography, love him. Let him know that you love him but hate what pornography does to the mind and spirit. Talk openly with him about the harmful long-term effects of viewing pornography (don't limit this to a one-time conversation), and help him set up an accountability plan. Here are a few possible ideas:

Set up a time to meet with your teen regularly. If your daughter has difficulty with pornography, this time can be a special mother/daughter bonding opportunity. If your son is struggling, make this a special "guy time" such as breakfast every Saturday morning or coffee after school every Tuesday.

Encourage him to schedule regular meeting times with a trusted adult such as a youth leader or pastor. Then follow up with your teen to see how his meetings are going. (Be careful not to force him to share every detail.)

Guide him through writing down a coping plan he can use when temptation arises. This may include going for a run or playing a sport, calling a friend, surrounding himself with other people, or journaling.

Make your home a safe haven for your teen. Do whatever is necessary to ensure that pornography and other influences are not finding a way into your home. As you take the time and effort to "put the fence" up and reinforce it with your relationship with your teen, you will keep out Satan and his tools.

chapter 11

Clothes, Hair, and Body Art: "It's Only a Tattoo"

You notice your daughter is beginning to create strange effects with her makeup, is wearing unusual jewelry around her neck, ankles, fingers, and wrists. She has more than one hole pierced in her ear. Maybe your son comes home with an earring. Some young people will actually come home with multiple piercings in their ears, their nose, their tongue, their eyebrows, and/or their navel. Others will just talk about it as a joke, just to see how mom and dad will respond.

It is shocking if your teen makes these physical changes overnight. You may grab her and say, "Who are you?! What have you done with my teenager?!?!"

the stranger upstairs

Realize this is still your child, although her hair, earrings, and clothes might look extremely bizarre. If your teen is already dressing like this or is beginning to get into it, it is imperative you emphasize your relationship and how much you care about her.

Be cautious about criticizing the look, the clothes, or jewelry. Although you may strongly, vehemently disagree (as I do), if your

Don't just talk about body piercings and hair all the time. Talk to her as a person— what she is thinking, feeling, and going through.

approval is based on how she looks, she will think your love is conditional.

Right now, more than ever, you must engage her in conversations that draw her heart back toward you. Don't just talk about body piercings and hair all the time. Talk to her as a person—what she is thinking, feeling, and going through. Get to know her all over again.

Should you be concerned about this kind of behavior? Absolutely, yes! Don't put it off as another phase your young person is going through. The mainstream of teenagers today is not behaving this way.

Look into the eyes and the heart of your young person to see what's going on inside. The problem is not the hair or body. The problem is the attitude that led her to do it—the need for peer acceptance and the need to "make a statement." What kind of statement is she making? Who influenced her to think that by doing this she would be making that statement? A band? A friend? Who are these friends?

Do not conform any longer to the pattern of this world, but be transformed by the renewing of your mind.
—Romans 12:2

When God looks at your teen, He does not look at all this stuff on the outside, but He definitely looks at what is going on inside.

What makes your teen feel like she has to dress in an outlandish way to communicate a point?

If the attitude your teen reflects is self-destructive—one of depression or rebellion against society, or one that says, "I don't care what you think, I'm going to do my own thing"—then obviously there is a real issue and a real problem.

Why do young people do this? They are identifying with some group—either a music group, a group of friends at school, at a hangout, on a sports team, or even in a youth group. Somehow it was put into their mind that if they changed their appearance, this particular group of people they regard as significant would accept them.

Please understand your teen will not see it like this. She thinks she is doing it to be an individual. Your job is not to convince your teen that you know better. You need to discover why she needs to feel accepted by that particular group. Talk to your teen; ask her about her friends (not in a condemning way); even encourage her to invite her friends over to your home. As you get to know your teen and her friends more and more, the *why* will become clearer.

Help your young person surround herself with the right kind of peers, not just whoever happens to be around. That is why it is so extremely important that you do not live under the same roof and eat at the same table without really knowing what is going on in her life. You have to help shape and influence the environment your young person grows up in.

Somehow your teen has woven herself into a group of people who are now very

Photo © Comstock

CULTURE

significant. It is important, then, that you do not just pass off her friends as stupid kids. "Why do they dress like that??!!" The more you think and talk that way, the more you will push your teen to identify with those kids and think you just don't understand.

It is important for you to know your teen's friends to show that you are not dismissing them without giving them a chance. At the same time, it is absolutely imperative that you help your young person find the right kind of friends to be around—those destined for success, who love God with all their hearts, and who are wholesome in every area of their lives.

Search out these young people and find ways to endear your teen to them. One way might be to meet with a great youth pastor in town. Talk with him about your teen. Ask him what his youth group might have to offer and what they could do to reach out and pull your young person in as a friend and a companion.

If your young person is a Christian and has been raised in church, she might be thinking, "I just want to reach out to other young people who are dressed like this." I caution you to be careful of that. Although it sounds legitimate on the surface, you still have great cause for concern.

She begins to talk to them, get to know them, and do all the right things to develop a relationship so she can evangelize them. But then she starts listening to them so much, she begins to defend them.

"You know what? These kids really have been misunderstood. There really are a lot of hypocrites out there. The church really doesn't understand them. I can't believe the church doesn't accept them. They went to this one church and they got so mistreated." She takes on these young people's offenses. Pretty soon she is more committed to and drawn to the people she is trying to reach out to than she is with Christian friends.

How far do we need to go to relate and reach out in order to effectively minister? Jesus did hang out with prostitutes. He hung out in bars. But He did not become like them. He didn't dress like

If your teen is dressing and acting dramatically different, should you immediately say, "Stop it right now!"?

them. He didn't even spend most of His time with them. He spent most of His time with His disciples.

When reaching out and ministering, it should be a ministry venture, not something your teen does on her own, hoping to survive spiritually. Do not play this down. She should not identify more with the group she is trying to reach out to than her group who loves God, has positive values, and a wholesome way of representing the Christian life.

If your teen is dressing and acting dramatically different, should you immediately say, "Stop it right now!"? It depends on where she is. If she is just barely starting to change, you know her heart is still with you, and she still loves God with all her heart, then yes, stop it right away—even if she doesn't understand.

If her heart is already gone and you say, "No more!" you could push her over the edge to say, "I'm going to do what I want to do anyway!" You have to be much more careful and diplomatic at how you woo her heart back toward you. You can enforce a rule at home, but as soon as she walks out the door, if her identity is still wrapped up with that group, your teen will put all the jewelry and earrings back on, and you have still lost her.

Some parents might say, "Well, as long as she doesn't do it around me, it's okay." No, it is not okay! That is not what you want. You want your teen's heart. You want a relationship. If she is already beyond that, you must be honest with yourself and realize you will have to be more tactful.

Begin to pull her in, get to know her friends, and diplomatically work through a strategy to get her involved with other devoted Christian young people. She may go through the motions—combing her hair right and wearing the right clothes in front of you. But if you have her *hair* and not her *heart*, you don't really have her. Talk it over with your spouse and with your pastor. See what the best way to approach the issue would be.

Even if your teen isn't dressing differently, talk about it. Make sure she understands that you won't allow it in your home. Spend time and talk, so her heart is drawn back to you. Don't even give her heart a chance to escape or to be drawn toward others who have succumbed to negative actions and attitudes of rebellion.

crisis

It's a call in the middle of the night. "Are you the parent of ——?" You have done your best to raise your child well, and now this—he's in trouble with the law, he tried to commit suicide, or he's drunk or high at a party.

How can a parent get through these times? And more importantly, how can a parent help prevent these kinds of crises?

It's about relationship. It's about accepting your teen for who he is but making sure he knows you do not agree with his actions. It's about communicating love like you have never done before. And it's about asking God to lead and guide you down paths you never thought you would go.

chapter 12
Suicide: "You'll Miss Me When I'm Gone"

Most teen suicides are not among the poor and unpopular. Many who both attempt and commit suicide are those you would least expect—those who look like they have everything going for them and are very popular.

And far more young people contemplate suicide than we might suspect. Suicide is the third leading cause of death among young adults and adolescents 15-24 years of age. Four out of five teens who attempt suicide have given clear warnings.[1]

signs of suicidal tendencies

Teens report that family problems, depression, and problems with friends and peer pressure contribute to suicidal thoughts and actions. We as parents must know the telltale signs of a young person considering suicide and what to do about it.

Signs of suicidal tendencies include:

❖ Changes in eating and sleeping habits

❖ Withdrawal from friends and family activities

❖ Violent or rebellious behavior (i.e. running away)

❖ Drug or alcohol abuse

❖ Fatigue or loss of energy

❖ Changes in hygiene

❖ Extreme anxiety

❖ Difficulty concentrating and a decline in schoolwork

❖ Feelings of hopelessness or desperation

❖ Loss of interest in pleasurable activities

❖ Feelings of worthlessness or guilt

❖ Giving away favorite possessions

❖ Speaking of death or suicide and comments like "I won't see you again."[2]

Seventy-five percent of suicide victims communicate their intention to someone beforehand. If you see any of these tendencies in your young person, take it seriously. Examine what is going on in his life and how you can help him get through it.[3]

what can you do?

What should you do if you see these signs in your young person's life?

Pray! I don't mean pray and then just hope things get better.

Really listen to your young person. Never underestimate the seriousness of a threat or suggested harm to herself.

I mean *pray a prayer of faith* over your young person. Rebuke the spirit of death from her life. Jesus said in John 10:10, "The thief comes only to steal and kill and destroy." If your young person is thinking in any way that life is not worth living and that she should end it, the enemy of her soul is trying to deceive. The devil is the one who wants your teen to die before her appointed time.

Say this prayer: "In Jesus' name, Satan, you cannot have my young person. I rebuke you in the name of Jesus. You stay away. She will live and not die. She will fulfill God's plan for her life." Pray a prayer of faith over her and deal with the core problem.

These aren't just words you can say and then expect the enemy to go running away with his tail between his legs. You have to pray until you know deep within your heart you have truly taken authority over every evil one. Jesus gave authority to His disciples to drive out evil spirits, and He has given that authority to us. (See Matthew 10:1 and Luke 10:19.)

Speak Scriptures over your teen and over your home. (See the end of this chapter for suggested Bible verses.) Go into her bedroom while she is at school or work and lay hands on and pray over her bed, clothes, and anoint with oil the doorpost and bedroom walls. Rebuke the enemy from her room and invite the Holy Spirit in. Place a hedge of divine protection around her physical being, actively taking authority.

If your young person has attempted, seriously contemplated, or talked about committing suicide, do not take this lightly. She is crying out for help! Get her into professional care right away for an evaluation. I would suggest a program like Rapha, which is a Christian counseling ministry.

Really listen to your young person. Never underestimate the seriousness of a threat or suggested harm to herself. Listen carefully to her emotions and plans. She may have planned a very specific way to end her life. If so, it is much more serious than you may have first thought.

Empathize with her. Don't just patronize, put down, or shrug off her feelings of loneliness, emptiness, and worthlessness. Empathizing means reflecting what she is saying with *your* own words, trying with all your heart to put yourself in her shoes.

Many times if you dismiss her feelings with, "You shouldn't feel like that, you should feel like this," your teen will feel like you are not really listening, not really connected, and not really caring about her. As you empathize, reinforce the fact that you recognize what she is feeling.

Just being there as a compassionate friend/parent can often diffuse a young person's sense of being all alone in her pain. If, in your eyes and in your heart, she sees you there every step of the way, she will not feel so isolated and alone.

Here are some specific things you can do:

Work on your relationship with her as it relates to different issues. Don't just be interested in talking about her thoughts of suicide, but rather talk to her about her life, heart, direction and goals, passion, and failures and successes. The best prevention for suicide is a healthy, strong relationship with parents and with other people. You will never really "arrive" in a relationship—it must be something you are continually working on.

Build self-worth. It is important to build your teen's self-worth, but not in a patronizing way. Don't just say, "Well, you're good at this, and you're good at that," every time she feels bad about herself. Begin building self-worth when you are not in a counseling session or in a deep conversation about suicide. When she says something witty, identify it. When she says something intelligent, comment on it. When she does something good, compliment her. You are looking for any reason to give her hope, taking baby steps along the way.

Instill hope. Suicidal people are generally people without hope. Give her hope and faith that things will get better, that God has a specific purpose for her. Teach your young person where suicidal thoughts come from. The enemy wants to destroy her life and soul, but God wants to give abundant life. (See John 10:10.) God wants to bless her, and all the hope and faith for an incredible life is found in Him alone. The people who know their God "shall be strong, and do exploits." (See Daniel 11:32 KJV.) "I can do all things through Christ who strengthens me." (Phil. 4:13 NKJV.) As you share Scriptures, it will build faith and hope in her heart that she can get through the cesspool of depression.

Teach coping skills. With all the pressures, temptations, frustrations, and confusion your teen faces, teach positive steps to take when she faces those crises; she does not have to feel hopeless. Share principles on how to live life so when she feels at the end of her rope, when she gets an F on a test, or when she doesn't do well in sports, she doesn't throw in the towel. You cannot expect to just sit down once and tell her some neat things to do that you read in a book. Coping skills must be reinforced constantly. "This is how you deal with life. This is how you deal

Photo © Comstock

CRISIS

with tough situations." Role play and talk through situations so that when she finds herself in one of those situations, she has the answers already prepared.

Develop a plan of action. If she starts considering suicide, what will you do? Develop a plan of action to deal with some of the most bothersome circumstances that make her feel hopeless. Help *her* develop a plan—how will she get out of this? How will she improve her situation? Don't just say, "Oh, you'll get over it," but help her find a way out by developing a plan of action. If a plan of action isn't obvious, research until you come up with one. Maybe a good plan would be to begin something new, fun, and interesting, such as horseback riding, a sport, or a project the two of you can work on together.

Finally, draw your teen into a personal commitment to prevent a suicide attempt. If she starts feeling depressed or thinking about suicide, she agrees to contact you. She agrees not to quit trying to contact you until she gets through. Keep a cell phone or pager with you, and agree to call back immediately.

Make yourself 100 percent available—if that means interrupting a meeting or getting off an important phone call, do it! *No situation is more important than supporting your son or daughter in this intense time.* Constantly reaffirm this commitment as you get together and talk.

Constantly let your teen know that God has a great plan for her life and that you are praying for her. Speak words of faith over her.

The ultimate plan is to instill hope, faith, and vision for the future. Constantly let your teen know that God has a great plan for her life and that you are praying for her. Speak words of faith over her.

Get her more concerned about the future and about reaching out and helping *others*. That will help draw her out of the depression. Pour your energy into helping her develop a vision for the future—a plan of faith and optimism. Ask God to birth a dream in your teen's heart of what He wants to do with her life. If she is consumed with God's plan and His hope for her future, she will be drawn further away from suicide and will begin to love and enjoy life.

Begin praying these Scripture verses over your teen:

> *No evil will befall you, nor will any plague come near*
> *your tent. For He will give His angels charge concerning*
> *you, to guard you in all your ways.*
> *—Psalm 91:10–11 NASB*

> *For He rescued us from the domain of darkness, and*
> *transferred us to the kingdom of His beloved Son.*
> *—Colossians 1:13 NASB*

> *No weapon that is formed against you will prosper.*
> *—Isaiah 54:17 NASB*

> *But you are a chosen people, a royal priesthood, a holy nation, a*
> *people belonging to God, that you may declare the praises of him*
> *who called you out of darkness into his wonderful light.*
> *—1 Peter 2:9*

> *But as for me and my household, we will serve the LORD.*
> *—Joshua 24:15b*

CRISIS

If you find yourself facing this situation, you also need strength and encouragement for yourself that only the Word of God can offer. Rely on the Holy Spirit to comfort and guide you in all your ways.

God is our refuge and strength, an ever-present help in trouble.
—Psalm 46:1

. . . the joy of the LORD is your strength.
—Nehemiah 8:10b

But thanks be to God! He gives us the victory through our Lord Jesus Christ.
—1 Corinthians 15:57

For our struggle is not against flesh and blood, but against the rulers, against the authorities, against the powers of this dark world and against the spiritual forces of evil in the heavenly realms.
—Ephesians 6:12

I will give you the keys of the kingdom of heaven; whatever you bind on earth will be bound in heaven, and whatever you loose on earth will be loosed in heaven.
—Matthew 16:19

When I am afraid, I will trust in you.
—Psalm 56:3

We demolish arguments and every pretension that sets itself up against the knowledge of God, and we take captive every thought to make it obedient to Christ.
—2 Corinthians 10:5

Yet this I call to mind and therefore I have hope: Because of the
Lord's great love we are not consumed, for his compassions
never fail. They are new every morning; great is your faithfulness.
—Lamentations 3:21–23

"For I know the plans I have for you," declares the Lord,
"plans to prosper you and not to harm you, plans to
give you hope and a future."
—Jeremiah 29:11

God has wonderful plans for your teen. He has a purpose for
her life. Stand on the promises of His Word, and you will have
the victory.

CRISIS

chapter 13 — Trouble with the Law: "It's the Police"

The phone rings. You search for the clock . . . 1:30 a.m.?! Who could possibly be calling at such an hour? You grab the phone and manage to grunt out a weak "Hello?" An official sounding voice on the other end asks, "Are you the parent of —— ?" You quickly respond, "Yes, I am."

In the ensuing few moments you discover your teen has broken the law and is in jail for the night. You have to think clearly. How should you respond? Who should you call? Should you try to bail him out or let him sit in the jail cell for one night? What should you do?

how to respond

Here are five principles to use in responding to a situation such as this.

1. Be compassionate. No matter how brokenhearted, mad, hurt, or angry you might be, it is important that you respond with compassion. Even though you don't like what he has done, your teen must know you still accept and love him.

No matter how brokenhearted, mad, hurt, or angry you might be, it is important that you respond with compassion.

Look at the story of the prodigal son in Luke 15:11–32. The son took his inheritance, went away, spent it all on prostitutes and parties, and became a disgrace to his family. Although his father was very wealthy, the son ended up in another country working as a slave and serving pigs. When he realized he had done wrong, he came running back to his father.

It's important to note what the father did. Even though he had been deeply hurt and his dreams and goals for his son had been shattered, as soon as he saw his son returning, he ran to him, threw his arms around him, and welcomed him home.

You need to respond with the same kind of attitude. No matter what your teen has done, he is still your child. Your love and acceptance should be unconditional — just as God's love is for us. (See John 13:34.)

At the same time, you want him to realize the gravity of the situation. You don't want him to think, "No big deal. It's really not that bad of a thing because they still love me." Let him know you don't approve of his actions. He has hurt his parents and maybe other family members. But also let him know you love him.

I heard a story of a well-known pastor whose son had been drifting further and further away from his family and from the Lord. After the boy made a huge mistake and landed in jail, the father went to visit him. Having a distant and cold relationship, the son wasn't sure how his father would respond. But the father looked into his son's eyes and said, "How can I help you?"

Those words tore down the wall standing between them. The son began to weep uncontrollably in his father's arms. Instead of condemning him or telling him he was no good, the father emphasized the fact that he was still his son and he still loved him. Their relationship was restored, and the son is no longer in jail or in trouble with the law.

2. Accept responsibility. "I know my child didn't really *mean* to do something wrong or illegal." Whether it was driving under the influence, armed robbery, petty theft, or vandalism, you are tempted to think, "He just got caught up with the wrong crowd."

This rationale is dangerous because it takes the responsibility off the young person. In essence, you believe it's not really his fault because he is a good kid—he was just with the wrong people at the wrong time. If it is not his responsibility, you can rationalize that he didn't do anything wrong.

Most parents think this is just a one-time thing. It's a fluke—an accident. You'll get him out of jail, off the hook, and everything will be fine—no problem. You must understand, it may be the first time in jail, but it certainly isn't the first step to getting into that situation.

Maybe you don't know your child as well as you thought you did. *If you dismiss this offense as an isolated incident, you're not seeing the picture for what it really is and you will not solve the problem.* You may get him out of jail, but the problem still remains.

What brought him to the point of stepping too close to the edge, doing something really stupid, and getting thrown in jail? What decisions could have been made differently for a

Photo © Stockbyte

CRISIS

better outcome? Instead of just getting him off the hook, see how you and your teen can keep this from happening again.

You are to influence and mold him. Make sure he is not hanging around friends that could get him into trouble. Don't allow him to stay out late or go to places that could result in a huge downfall. And remember, *you* are his example. Your own actions and standards speak louder than any lecture can.

Instead of trying to deny that your teen is really like this, get to know him. Make your teen your first priority. Develop a relationship with him. Allow him to provide you with insight as to why he wants to do the things he does. He isn't a bad person—he simply needs direction and guidance.

3. Accept the consequences. Our first reaction is to get him out of trouble. We don't want him to embarrass us. We don't want him to mess up his life. We don't want him to have a criminal record. We can't stand the thought of having him fully pay the price and suffer the consequences. Other people can pay for what they do, but not our child!

Be careful if you are thinking like this. It may very well damage your young person more than it will help him. He has committed a serious infraction, or he wouldn't be in jail. If you bail him out now, you might be bailing him out the rest of his life.

It is important he accepts responsibility and pays the consequences, which will most likely deter him from further wrongdoing. Dr. James Dobson calls this *tough love*.[1]

It is important he accepts responsibility and pays the consequences, which will most likely deter him from further wrongdoing.

CRISIS

In our society, if someone robs a bank and asks the Lord to forgive him, He does, but the robber still has to face the consequences. God's grace and forgiveness is there for us, but consequences still remain. God wants us to be responsible people.

I was involved with a family whose teenage son had been part of an armed robbery. During the robbery, the store owner was killed. These Christian parents didn't know what to do. Their options were to have their son turn himself in or to have him flee the country, since he hadn't been caught.

If he turned himself in, they knew the law would take its full course. If he fled the country, he would be running the rest of his life. He decided to turn himself in. The parents got the best attorney they could find and went to court.

Through it all, this young man really turned his life over to the Lord. He did go to jail, but he stayed close to the Lord throughout his jail time. He experienced time in jail as a consequence to his crime, but he also experienced God's compassion and grace. Now, out of jail and in full-time ministry, this situation has been turned around and has brought glory and honor to God. (See Romans 8:28.)

If it had been possible, these parents would have tried to get their son completely off the hook so he wouldn't have to serve jail time. But it wasn't possible, and it was definitely not wise.

In some cases, an attorney can get a young person off on a lesser charge or completely prevent him from serving time or probation, yet the teenager hasn't learned anything. Having to face tough consequences serves as a huge reminder and milestone for the rest of a teen's life that this is something he does not want to repeat!

4. Involve your pastor. Ask your pastor to visit your son or daughter. Ask for his counsel on what went wrong and search the Bible on what to do next. You don't want to go through this situation alone. You need a few close Christian friends and the leaders

If he learns to honor authorities, leaders, rules, regulations, and laws, his life will be blessed.

of the church praying for your family and encouraging you. Don't fight this battle all alone. Yes, it is embarrassing, but people are going to find out anyway. You might as well tell those who love you so they can stand with you and pray for you.

5. Incorporate preventive measures. If your child has not broken the law, you can take some preventive measures. The first one is *discipline*. We need to teach our children about discipline when they are young. This is more than spankings—it is learning to live a disciplined life.

Does your teen know what your standards are? *Teach him to abide faithfully by the rules you have set at home as well as the rules society sets up as our governing laws.* If he learns to honor authorities, leaders, rules, regulations, and laws, his life will be blessed.

Teach him the difference between right and wrong. Set disciplinary measures and be prepared to follow through. Even as a teen in your home, he needs to know he will pay a price if he goes beyond what you permit. That price may be no television, no social activities, or no telephone privileges. If you teach him there are consequences for his actions, beginning in his childhood and all the way through his teen years, he will understand that he has to suffer those consequences.

Teach him by your example to *respect* and *obey* laws and authority figures. Do you bad-mouth the teacher, the coach, the instructor, or the principal? Do you speak ill of them behind their backs? Do you observe the governing laws set for you? If your child's teacher carries out disciplinary measures, are you quick to come to the defense of your child, believing your child could do absolutely nothing wrong? If so, this is damaging your child!

Everyone must submit himself to the governing authorities, for there is no authority except that which God has established. The authorities that exist have been established by God. Consequently, he who rebels against the authority is rebelling against what God has instituted, and those who do so will bring judgment on themselves. . . . Therefore, it is necessary to submit to the authorities, not only because of possible punishment but also because of conscience.
—Romans 13:1–2, 5

Laws, rules, and regulations are set up by God to establish order. We stay out of trouble because we know there will be a price to pay, but also because disobedience is considered rebellion against God. Teach your teen that submitting to authority is not only the right and honorable thing to do, it also is the godly thing to do.

What happens when the court proceedings are over, when he is out of jail, or when the probation time is up? Is it really over? Hopefully this incident has served as a wake-up call.

Are you still showing unconditional love? This time can be the beginning of a brand-new journey for you and your teen. Spend time doing fun things with him. Listen to discover what is in his heart. Look for opportunities to teach the principles that will keep him close to God and away from further legal trouble. Help him find God's will so he can begin to experience His richest blessings.

CRISIS

chapter 14

Rape: "All I Wanted Was a Kiss"

Far more often than we would like to admit—often in the form of what is called "date rape,"—a young woman is pushed beyond her comfort level. Date or acquaintance rape accounts for 80 to 90 percent of sexual assaults.[1]

She has said "no" a couple of times and is with someone she knows. But when it's all said and done, she is not really sure what happened. She never intended to let it happen and not really sure if she allowed it, since there was no screaming or fighting involved. She feels violated. She is embarrassed and ashamed. In most cases, she is afraid to tell anyone, especially her parents.

One young woman said,

> "I lied to my parents and told them I was going to a
> friend's house. I went out drinking with my guy
> friends and then dancing. One of them got mad and
> beat me until I was unconscious. I had asked the
> other guys to take me home, but they ended up
> taking me somewhere else. Three of them raped me.
> My parents grounded me for six months and never
> took me to the doctor or even talked to me about it."

CRISIS

Listen to what other young people have said:

> **"I had sex with my boyfriend. They didn't**
> **know it wasn't my choice. My mother told me**
> **that I had completely ruined my life**
> **and wouldn't speak to me for a long time."**

> **"After I had been raped, I wish my parents had not**
> **made me feel guilty for 'allowing it' to happen.**
> **I wish they had been there for love and support."**

Only 20 percent of sexual assaults are by strangers. In San Diego, four out of five rape victims reported that their perpetrators were acquaintances or friends. In a recent survey, 56 percent of high school girls and 76 percent of boys thought forced sex was acceptable sometimes. Fifty-one percent of boys and 41 percent of girls said that forced sex was acceptable if the boy "spent a lot of money" on the girl. Sixty-five percent of boys and 47 percent of girls said it was acceptable for a boy to rape a girl if they had dated for more than six months.[2]

the truth about rape

You can't believe everything you hear—especially about rape. What are some of the most common myths about this crime?

Myth: Rape is no big deal. It's just sex.
Truth: Rape is not just sex—it's a violent crime that uses a sexual weapon. Rape causes long-term emotional and physical damage. The effects of rape cannot be ignored, and victims should seek professional Christian counseling.

Myth: It's not really rape if you're attacked by someone you know.

Truth: Four out of five rapists are known by the victims. Acquaintances are as capable of committing rape as anyone.[3]

Myth: Date rape is not really a rape because the woman agreed to go out with the man, and therefore led him to believe she was sexually interested.

Truth: Any forced sex is rape, whether the violator is friend, familiar face, or foe. When a woman agrees to go out with a man, she is not automatically agreeing to any sexual activity. No matter how much money the man spends on the woman, or how attracted he thinks he is to her, to force sexual activity is to rape her.

Myth: The woman always has to try to physically fight the man off before it's considered rape. The charge is based on the strength of her resistance.

Truth: In many states, a man who persists when a woman verbally says "no" is considered a rapist. Many states also say a woman doesn't have to say "no"; it's rape if she doesn't specifically say "yes" or if she is too intoxicated or otherwise unable to make a sound judgment. Some organizations are pressing for new laws to charge men with rape when they psychologically coerce women into unwanted sex.

Photo © Comstock

CRISIS

Myth: The perpetrator acted out of love.

Truth: Love respects, is kind, and gives. Love does not hurt another or demand to control that person.

Jesus came to take the brokenhearted in His hands, love them, pick up the pieces of their hearts and put them back together again.

Myth: Only young, pretty women are victims.

Truth: Rape happens to women, and occasionally men, of all ages, sizes, races, and appearances. Because rape is a violent crime, it is not one caused by the temptation of beauty.

Myth: The rapist is simply oversexed.

Truth: The rapist is an emotionally off-balanced person who uses forced sex to gain control.

Myth: The rapist is a child who cannot control his new sexual feelings.

Truth: No matter his age, the rapist knows what he is doing. He is acting not from sexual desire but from misplaced anger.

Myth: The victims asked for it.

Truth: No one asks for something horrible to happen to her. No matter what the victim does or says, no one has the right to abuse that person.

Myth: Women have secret fantasies about being raped.

Truth: Men who believe this myth have a misconception about the emotional make-up of women.

Myth: If the woman says "no" but lets you kiss her, she means "yes" or wants you to persuade her.

Truth: No means no. Just because a woman feels attracted to a man and lets him kiss her does not mean she wants to be raped. If she's having a hard time putting her head above her hormones or emotions, the man still does not have the right to take advantage of her.

Myth: It's not really rape unless it's intercourse.
Truth: In most states, any kind of forced sexual activity is considered rape, including anal or oral sex and other sexual liberties.[4]

If you find yourself in a situation where your daughter has been violated, what should you do?

In *Parents and Teenagers*, Janice Short gives seven practical guidelines (and I have added one of my own) for responding to the shock of your daughter's rape:

1. Believe her story.
2. React to the news with a nonjudgmental and supportive attitude.
3. Don't treat your daughter like she is damaged property.
4. Talk openly about the rape.
5. Avoid being overprotective or patronizing.
6. Accept her emotions, even if you don't understand them.
7. Seek counseling for yourself and your daughter.[5]
8. Be caring and loving toward your daughter.

Contact the authorities. Go about this carefully so as to protect the privacy of your daughter and your family. Whether or not it seems like your daughter had an active part in luring this guy, the authorities should still be contacted. A police report should be made. That guy should be stopped before he does it to someone else.

Too many times a parent blames the daughter and says, "You weren't really raped. You wanted it to happen. You were being too promiscuous. You led that guy on." Many teens have unsupportive

CRISIS

parents, so they are afraid to tell them what happened, hiding behind silent sadness and deep hurt. This tragedy is compounded by the fact that they feel they cannot talk to anyone about it.

If your daughter does come to you, reach out your arms and let her know you love her. You believe her. You are going to stand with her. She is going to struggle with feeling dirty, unworthy, and impure as a result of this. Completely love and accept your daughter.

Jesus said in Luke 4:18 (NKJV) that He came "to heal the brokenhearted." That is, Jesus came to take the brokenhearted in His hands, love them, pick up the pieces of their hearts and put them back together again. That is the role you need to play as a parent.

If she has not come to you about a situation like this, it is particularly important for you to pay attention to her attitudes and behavior regarding any and all dating experiences. First of all, make sure you have prayed about your teen's dating relationships. You must have that inner peace from God.

Get well acquainted with the person your daughter is about to go out with—not just his name. Spend time with him. Have him come over to the house a few times for dinner before allowing your daughter to go out with him. You need to be confident he has the character to treat your daughter with dignity and respect—or don't you dare let him take her out!

Once he has passed the approval process, which may take several weeks or even months, be sure to know all of their plans for the evening. Know where they will be and what time your daughter will be home. Maybe even have your daughter call and check in the first few times they go out.

Be sure, either that night or the next morning, to talk about how the date went—look into her eyes, look at her demeanor, see how she carries herself. Is she really herself with you? You are watching for signs. Maybe something happened that she is ashamed of or doesn't want to tell you about. Not that you are trying to be a detective, but if a tragedy has happened, you want to be the first one to rescue her and help her pick up the pieces.

the worst scenario

Contact your pastor and youth pastor. Get people praying for your daughter and family. God can use those in leadership at your church to help bind up broken hearts, put the pieces back together, and be a source of encouragement as you walk through this process of restoring wholeness to your daughter and your family.

Take your daughter to a trusted physician. Rape has long-term physical effects, and in some cases, diseases or pregnancy can even result. Going to the doctor may be embarrassing for your daughter, so encourage her and explain that her physical hurt is not her fault.

Find a good Christian counselor or one of the pastoral staff at your church to talk through the painful issues of forgiveness, wholeness, and purity. Too many parents think, "Just get over it. Put a bandage on it. It will be okay." They would rather put it out of their minds and pretend it didn't happen. It didn't happen to you, but it did happen to your daughter, and she can't pretend it didn't.

CRISIS

Most importantly, let her know how much God loves her!

To bring freedom and wholeness to her, know that it takes time for complete restoration. Don't get impatient with the process. Ask God to fill you with His grace, mercy, and love as you walk through this together and come out a stronger family.

Most importantly, let her know how much God loves her! He is not ashamed of her for what happened. He wants to comfort, love, and give her peace. Although it may seem like it to her, her life is not over. He has great plans and good things for her. Encourage her to seek the Lord and turn to Him in this time of trouble.

He who dwells in the shelter of the Most High will
rest in the shadow of the Almighty.
—Psalm 91:1

This is love: not that we loved God, but that he loved us and sent
his Son as an atoning sacrifice for our sins.
—1 John 4:10

God is our refuge and strength, an ever-present help in trouble.
—Psalm 46:1

Brothers, I do not consider myself yet to have taken hold of it. But
one thing I do: Forgetting what is behind and straining toward
what is ahead, I press on toward the goal to win the prize for
which God has called me heavenward in Christ Jesus.
—Philippians 3:13–14

He lifted me out of the slimy pit, out of the mud and mire; he set
my feet on a rock and gave me a firm place to stand. He put a
new song in my mouth, a hymn of praise to our God. Many will
see and fear and put their trust in the LORD.
—Psalm 40:2–3

Your daughter and your family will forever remember how you respond in this time of crisis. Getting mad at yourself, the perpetrator, or your daughter will not resolve the issue.

Respond with mercy, understanding, and compassion, and she will remember. As she journeyed down this road to recovery, she will see how her mother and father wrapped themselves around her heart and life like a protective cocoon.

chapter 15

Drugs: "Something Passed around at the Party"

In a world that glamorizes drug use, it is easy to see why teens are drawn to using them. Between television, movies, and peers at school, our kids are bombarded with the fantasy drugs seem to offer. Drug use is rising among teens. The University of Michigan surveyed 50,000 students across the country and found that one in four teens uses some type of drug before high school. The study's director believes that the increase is largely due to the entertainment industry's glamorization of drugs.[1]

Marijuana is the most commonly used illicit drug in the United States.[2] In fact, a survey of students in grades eight through twelve shows that 23 percent of eighth graders have tried marijuana at least once.[3] By twelfth grade, nearly 50 percent of teens have tried marijuana at least once, and about 24 percent are current users.[4] Every day in America, 500 adolescents begin using drugs. Thirty-nine percent of fourth-graders say that "using drugs is a big problem among kids our age."[5]

A group of 12- and 17-year-olds were asked the question, "Why do your peers use drugs?"

Reason	Respondents Age 12	Respondents Age 17
To be cool	49 percent	11 percent
Friends doing it	24 percent	25 percent
To feel good	9 percent	23 percent
Drug abuse in family	7 percent	4 percent
Stress relief	6 percent	22 percent
Personal problems	3 percent	7 percent
To rebel	1 percent	6 percent[6]

Some causes of drug use and abuse are peer pressure, sexual or physical abuse, parental neglect, parental example, and the need to escape. Some of the physical ramifications of drug use include leukemia, heart attack, infertility, tissue damage, and malnutrition.[7]

"I only smoked [pot] for a few months. Now I'm on drugs for the rest of my life. I thought marijuana was no big deal," says Kevin West, age 19. He shot himself playing Russian roulette while high on pot and is now paralyzed on his left side and must take anti-seizure medications daily.[8]

How do you know if your teen is using drugs—and if he is, what do you do? First, talk to him. If you don't know how to start the conversation, try something like, "We've never really talked about this before. I'm pretty nervous but I really need to know what you think about teens using drugs and drinking." Or, "I keep hearing the slogan, 'Just say "no" to drugs.' Does that really work? Maybe we can come up with some other things that will help."

CRISIS

Some parents even find that conversations with their teens are easier to start while driving in the car. If it's difficult to talk about drugs while in the same room as your teen, you may want to write each other letters or emails to begin the conversation and break the ice.

While a relationship and meaningful conversation are most vital whether or not your teen uses drugs, it's good to be aware of signs that frequently accompany drug use.

- ✤ Change in mood or behavior characterized by withdrawal from family, school and social activity.

- ✤ Changes in school performance and behavior.

- ✤ Changes in friends and a reluctance to bring them home to meet you.

- ✤ Unexplained injuries.[9]

If you find your teen is using drugs, I suggest the following steps:

1. **Make sure you let him know you still love him, even though you do not like the behavior.** Distinguish between his behavior and the person.
2. **Think through the discipline you want to use.** As a teen, he is too old for spanking. Respect and retain his dignity as a human being. There are ways you can discipline such as restricting favorite movies or television shows, taking items out of his room for a certain period of time, not allowing him to have certain food, or restricting phone calls and activities. Do not respond out of anger! Your goal is to make him feel the pain for what he has done so he will want to change in that area.

CRISIS

3. **Develop a dialogue about the drug issue.** Do not just tell
him, "Never do it again!" and the next time you talk about it is
the next time you catch him doing it. Discuss the drug issue
in a number of different ways:

   ❧ Use statistics. Let him know the physical consequences from a medical standpoint.

   ❧ Teach your teen why it is wrong. As in alcohol abuse,
   he is giving the control of his brain over to a drug.
   The drug dictates what he does and what he says.
   He is choosing to be irresponsible by letting drugs
   control him.

4. **Speak with a Christian counselor.** He can help you decide
if your teen should participate in a rehabilitation program.
The real danger here is not only physical danger, but also *spiritual danger*. In the Old Testament the word for "sorcery" is
pharmakeia. Sorcery involved talking with demons and evil
spirits. *Pharmakeia* is where we get our word "pharmacy." It
was directly related to drug abuse. Sorcerers would smell
incense, as they still do today in some parts of the world, and
it would distort their brain. As a result, sorcery and interaction
with demons was possible.

Teach your teen that as he relinquishes control of his mind to
a drug, he no longer has the resources to stand against the world
of evil spirits. So many people have become oppressed, depressed,

CRISIS

If your teen is doing drugs,
it is imperative you pray
over him in the name of
Jesus and rebuke the devil.

or possessed by an evil spirit as a result of doing drugs. They can't figure out why they are depressed, and angry all the time. By letting their guard down, they have been invaded by something they never asked for and were never even aware of.

This is not just a matter of saying, "Now, young man, be a good boy and don't do those drugs." This is a matter of keeping the world of evil spirits out of your teen's heart, mind, and life and keeping a strong resistance against the enemy.

> Our county is a place where the median average price for a home is about 800K. With all of its affluence and wealth, this county is one of the least evangelized counties in America, has the highest rate of breast cancer in women, has an alcohol and a meth epidemic and, on a positive note, has a teen population who are hungry for Christ. The enemy knows this and is doing what he does: kill, steal, and destroy. It's time for revival!
>
> —*Parent of a Teen*

If your teen is doing drugs, it is imperative you pray over him in the name of Jesus and rebuke the devil. If your teen has not given his life to the Lord, tell him how important it is, now more than ever, to invite Jesus into his life to forgive him. Then take a stand against the enemy. Have him pray, "In the name of Jesus, any evil spirit or any demon that may have tried to oppress me or possess me as a result of letting my self-control and my guard down, I rebuke you. You have no part of my life, in Jesus' name. Amen."

I encourage you to begin the process of ongoing education about drugs and why they are wrong. Help your teen to

CRISIS

understand the *why* rather than just giving him a *no*. You will be amazed at how responsive your young person will be if you are telling him *why*. Together, develop a coping plan—steps he will take when he feels peer pressure to do drugs. As part of his plan, encourage him to contact you anytime he is in an uncomfortable situation and make yourself available to him at anytime of the day or night.

Give him an arsenal of reasons and information why not to take drugs so that he can convince his friends that what they are doing is totally irrational and uncalled for. When it becomes *his* conviction, and not just *yours*, your teen will be unstoppable.

chapter 16

Tobacco: "Just a Couple Puffs"

Cigarette smoking went from being a simple pastime to a mark of independence, rebellion, and maturity among teenagers in the 1950s. Today's teenagers are no different. Cigarette advertising is marketed toward young people, as in the case of Joe Camel, who was banned from advertisements.

The tobacco companies know they won't make much money from teens while they are young, but if they can get them to experiment with smoking, the potential exists to make money off them throughout their lives. Why do young people use tobacco? They are trying to communicate:

"I belong."

"I am grown up."

"I am tough."

"I am angry."

The final reason young people smoke is that it is truly an addiction.[1] Eighty-five percent of all smokers wish they could quit. According to the American Lung Association, at least 4.5 million U.S. adolescents are cigarette smokers. Approximately 90 percent of smokers begin smoking before the age of 21. A 2001 survey of high school students found that the overall prevalence of current cigarette use was 28 percent.[2]

Chewing tobacco is also on the rise. The harmful effects of chewing tobacco include: cancer of the mouth and pharynx, leukoplakia (white sores in the mouth that can lead to cancer), gum recession, bone loss around the teeth, abrasion of teeth, and bad breath.[3]

Have you found cigarette butts in her room? Have you smelled smoke on her breath or clothes? Does she seem to have all the right excuses for smelling smoky when she comes in at night? What should you do if you suspect your teenager is using tobacco, either once in a while or all the time?

Maybe you're thinking, "Well, at least I don't smell alcohol on her breath . . . or at least she's not pregnant. If smoking is all my young person is doing, then I can be thankful for that." Can you really? How do you know that is the only thing she is doing? How should you approach the subject with your young person? Here are some suggestions:

First, you should be concerned not only with the act of smoking, which ultimately can be very harmful physically, but also your relationship with your teen. The goal is not to catch her red-handed or prove beyond a shadow of a doubt she is smoking just so you can get in her face. The goal is to have an incredibly great relationship with your teen so you can continue teaching her how to live a responsible life.

If you have that best-friend relationship with her, the ideal situation is that she would come to you if she were even tempted with a cigarette, not to mention if she had actually tried one. So if she hasn't told you, you need to work on improving your

Most young people don't start smoking because one day that idea pops into their minds.

relationship—not just proving or disproving the fact that she is or is not smoking.

The next major issue concerning smoking is the people with whom your young person is hanging around—those who are most likely luring her into it. Most young people don't start smoking because one day that idea pops into their minds. Whether on purpose or by accident, they have surrounded themselves with people who are attracted to smoking, for whatever reason. Something about having a cigarette in their hands, blowing smoke out their mouths, and hanging around others who do the same brings a sense of camaraderie and belonging. It means your young person has grown closer to a group who smoke than she has to you.

How well do you know her friends? Do you know who she associates with at school and after school? At this age friendships are extremely important. Young people place an incredible amount of value on their peers' opinion of them. It can be desperately important for them to belong to a certain group because their identities are wrapped up in their friends.

If this is the case, no amount of lecturing about how bad smoking is and no amount of punishment for smoking will do much good. The power of peer pressure is considerably more influential because they desperately want to belong. And "belonging" to that group by smoking could be the beginning of worse things to come.

It may start with smoking and then progress to parties and drug use. The road to destruction can be a difficult one to get off.

CRISIS

Of course your teen will not agree. She will say, "Sure. I'm smoking a cigarette and the next thing you know I'm a drug addict! I don't think so!" It won't make any sense, and she will think you are overreacting.

What do you do? You begin to investigate your young person's friends. Get to know these people. Invite them over to the house. Find out what makes them tick. See if they are the type of people you really want rubbing off on your young person.

If not, it may be time to take drastic measures. It may be time for you to move to a different part of the city or to a different state. It may be time for you to find another church if the young people at church smoke. (If you think none of the young people in the youth group smoke, don't kid yourself!) It might mean enrolling your teen in another school.

Do what it takes to salvage the teenage years while you can. However, just making these changes is not the solution. Unless she has a change of heart, your young person will find the same type of peers with the same attitudes wherever she goes.

You will have to take overt steps to get her in the right peer group. That may mean finding a fired-up youth group, sending her on a mission trip, or getting her to a youth conference or camp. Get her in an exciting, spiritual environment and keep her there until she catches what's there.

Notice she didn't start smoking the first day at a new school. She had to spend time with those people and get familiar with them before she started smoking or having the bad

Do what it takes to salvage the teenage years while you can.

attitude. The same applies to catching the fire of God—the fire of wanting to do what is right, holy, true, and truthful. You have to help her become comfortable there until she begins to make some real friends.

You can show her pictures of people with lung cancer and of people who have chewed tobacco for 20 years. It might serve as enough shock value to wake her up and make her realize that smoking is not all the "fun" it's cracked up to be.

Show your young person scriptures like 1 Corinthians 6:19, which says, ". . . Your body is a temple of the Holy Spirit . . ." If she has given her life to Jesus, God lives inside her body. *He lives in her.* She needs to treat her body like a temple. God created her body to function a certain way, and the more she uses tobacco, the more she is destroying the very thing God gave her. Hopefully this will serve as some motivation to those genuinely interested in the things of God and in wanting to serve Him.

Above all, do not pass off smoking as a phase she is going through. "It will pass. It's not that big of a deal." In too many cases, smoking is the first step toward a much bigger deal. Her present relationships with you and her friends are an indication whether she is going down the wrong path. Take action now!

CRISIS

chapter 17
Alcohol: "Everyone Drinks a Little"

It started by going to a few parties with friends. You thought he would never drink—so did he. It may be just a few beers, it may be getting drunk once in a while, or it may be a serious drinking problem.

Seventy-nine percent of students say it is easy to get alcohol. Seventy-seven percent say alcohol is common at parties. Forty-one percent say some of their friends have a problem with alcohol, and 22 percent have ridden in a car with someone who has been drinking.[1]

what can you do?

Before you fly off the handle and destroy the possibility of a relationship with your young person, take a deep breath. Realize he is still the same person on the inside as he was before he began drinking. He is still your child and will remember the way you respond to this crisis for the rest of his life.

Ask yourself this question: "How much have I really taught them about drinking—the physical dangers and the emotional effects?" It is easy for parents simply to tell their young person not to drink, but it is another thing to teach him based upon principles.

Do not discipline out of anger! But think about what will make your teen feel the sting of having gone against your wishes.

While expressing that, although you do not approve of or like the behavior, you still love and appreciate him, it is important he understands both are very true. Just because you do not like the behavior does not mean you do not love him. It seems like a small distinction to us, but it is huge to a young person. Jesus did things like that all the time, as with the woman who was caught in adultery. He did not condemn her or put her down, but at the same time, He was very clear. He told her, "Go and sin no more." (See John 8:11 NJKV.)

Think about the disciplinary measures you need to implement. Don't just say, "Don't do that again." If he is going against your wishes, there ought to be a price to pay—working around the house, giving up privileges, restricting phone calls, etc. Tell him drinking is wrong and you do not want him doing it, but use consequences that will make him think. Do not discipline out of anger! But think about what will make your teen feel the sting of having gone against your wishes.

Educate your teen by sharing the following:

According to research, in 2001, more than half a million people were injured in crashes where police reported that alcohol was present—an average of one person injured approximately every minute.[2] Find some local stories of young people who were driving drunk and have gone to jail or were involved in tragic car accidents.

The Bible says in Proverbs 20:1, "Wine is a mocker and beer a brawler; whoever is led astray by them is not wise." The Bible plainly tells us that if you drink, you are going to be mocked. You are going to do stupid things—things that you may not remember and will likely regret.

God designed you to be in charge of your mind and in charge of your life. In Genesis 1:26 God says He gives us "rule over the fish of the sea and the birds of the air, over the livestock, over all the earth, and over all the creatures that move along the ground." He gave us dominion. He put us in charge of the world.

When you choose to drink, you give charge of your brain over to a drug. A drug is now in charge of you. Alcohol is now in charge of your brain. You are not taking responsibility for your life. You begin the process of slowly flushing your life down the toilet.

Wine is a mocker. Ultimately, the very alcohol you drink will end up mocking you and laughing in your face because it destroyed your life. You become a slave to it. Romans 6:16 says, "Don't you know that when you offer yourselves to someone to obey him as slaves, you are slaves to the one whom you obey— whether you are slaves to sin, which leads to death, or to obedience, which leads to righteousness?"

If you choose to obey and submit yourself to alcohol, you are no longer a slave to the Lord. You are no longer the master of your own destiny. You have become the slave of a fermented grape. Drinking may seem like the tough, cool thing to do, but ultimately you degenerate as a human being.

Photo © PhotoDisc

CRISIS

Discuss object lessons as you drive by bars or when you see alcohol in stores. Say things like, "There are people in there right now who are hurting and broken, not knowing that the real answer is to give their lives to God. There are people in there who could have been doctors, lawyers, authors, or inventors, but they flushed their potential down the toilet of alcohol."

Develop this process of teaching, training, and constantly expounding on the craziness and foolishness of using alcohol, and it will help your teen develop his own conviction. He will refrain from drinking because he sees alcohol for what it truly is.

chapter 18

Sexual Activity: "I Don't Want to Be Old-Fashioned"

If you are reading this chapter, your heart is probably sick and broken to know your little girl or young man is no longer sexually pure. The thing you dreaded happening has happened, or you have good reason to believe it may have happened. Before you get overwhelmed with, "If I had only . . ." thoughts, let me say that there are a lot of actions we can all take to be better parents.

Remorse about your own performance as a parent will not help your teen. What is important now is how you respond to the situation, that you rescue and salvage the relationship between you and your teenage son or daughter.

Listen to what some teens have said:

> "I am sexually active, and
> I feel like it is unstoppable."

> "My mom knows that I am sexually active,
> but she doesn't do anything about it."

> "All my mom did was take me to the doctor
> and have them talk to me about sex."

According to the Alan Guttmacher Institute, the average age of first teenage sex is 15.8 years.[1] Yet, 67 percent of sexually experienced teens (77 percent of girls and 60 of boys) wish they had waited longer to become sexually active.[2]

why teens have sex

Why do teens have sex? Girls and guys responded differently:

- Sixty-one percent of girls and 23 percent of boys cite pressure from the dating partner.

- Fifty-nine percent of girls and 51 percent of boys say it happens because they think they are ready.

- Forty-five percent of girls have sex because they want to be loved, while 28 percent of boys give that reason.

- Thirty-eight percent of girls are afraid of being teased about their virginity, compared to 43 percent of boys.[3]

In *Josh McDowell's Handbook on Counseling Youth*, McDowell gives several reasons for premarital sex:

Educational and Societal Messages. The messages thrown at young people by society in general and by educational programs in particular are reasons for sexual activity.

Low Level of Religious Commitment. More frequent attendance at religious services leads to more restrictive attitudes concerning premarital sex and less sexual experience.

Family Structure. The effects of divorce and other family disruption and separation have been documented in numerous studies. One of those effects is sexual activity.

Poor Sex Education at Home. Kids who don't find the answers at home often learn the answers by painful experience. In the words of one teen, "Teenagers are ignorant about what they're doing. All they know is that they were made with certain body parts, so they might as well find out what they're used for. Sort of like test driving a car just to see how well it performs."

Relational Needs. Many young people are uncertain of their parents' love.

Early Dating. The younger a girl begins to date, the more likely she is to have sex before graduating from high school. It is also true of boys and girls who go steady in the ninth grade. Of girls who begin dating at age 12, 91 percent had sex before graduation—compared to 56 percent who dated at 13, 53 percent who dated at 14, 40 percent who dated at 15, and 20 percent who dated at 16.

Peer Pressure. A study of a thousand teens showed that 76 percent would go far enough sexually to feel experienced and not feel left out.

Alcohol and Drugs. The use of alcohol and other drugs hastens sexual involvement.

Desire for a Child. Although most youth want desperately to avoid becoming pregnant, some teenage girls are motivated to become sexually active by a desire to have a child. She may feel so bad about herself and so unloved that she tries intentionally to have a child, someone she can love and who will love her back.[4]

According to 61 percent of the girls, the top reason they have sex is a "boy pressuring them."[5]

When a young person reaches puberty, it's safe to assume the struggle with sexual desires has begun. You can make a number of observations to determine the intensity of your child's struggle.

CRISIS

How does your son look at girls? Have you found pornographic magazines in your teen's possession? How does your daughter talk about boys? Does she emphasize only their looks and not their personalities? When with a member of the opposite sex, does your teen constantly need to be touching?[6]

how should you respond?

How should you respond to your teen when you find out she is no longer sexually pure? First, *be sure you show her your love and care.* Sometimes the reaction can be so intense from a parent's hurt, anger, and frustration that it pushes the young person further away until there is little hope of regaining her moral strength. Do not be so shocked that you fail to remember that inside that body is the real person. Most times the body has grown up a lot faster than the mind, will, and emotions. Right now your teen needs direction, someone who believes in her, and someone who is willing to help her gain wisdom in the situation.

Next, take a deep breath and answer a few difficult questions. How much have you talked to your teen about sex? How much have you really explained? How many moral issues have you discussed? If you made it very clear to her that sex before marriage and any kind of petting before marriage is wrong, have you told her why? Our culture promotes sexual indiscretion and sleeping around. In fact, 36 percent of 15- to 17-year-olds report that they've had oral sex.[7] And "half of these teens do not identify oral sex as sex, according to 2003 surveys."[8]

With all that bombardment of the world's values, what have we done to bombard our children with the right message?

With all that bombardment of the world's values, what have we done to bombard our children with the right message? There is not only a false perception among teens about what is morally right, but there is a misunderstanding as to what's even "normal." Teens overestimate their peers' sexual experiences. In grades nine through twelve, 68 percent of students said their peers have had sex. According to a 2001 Youth Risk Behavior Survey conducted by the Center for Disease Control, only 46 percent of teens in those grades have had sex.[9] Your teen is likely feeling pressure that may not even exist as strongly as she perceives it.

Talk to your teen about God's plan for purity and *why* His plan works.

> *It is God's will that you should be sanctified:*
> *that you should avoid sexual immorality.*
> *—1 Thessalonians 4:3*

> *The body is not meant for sexual immorality,*
> *but for the Lord, and the Lord for the body.*
> *—1 Corinthians 6:13b*

> *Flee from sexual immorality. All other sins a man commits are*
> *outside his body, but he who sins sexually sins against his own*
> *body. Do you not know that your body is a temple of the Holy*
> *Spirit, who is in you, whom you have received from God? You are*
> *not your own; you were bought at a price.*
> *Therefore honor God with your body.*
> *—1 Corinthians 6:18–20*

We must help our teens understand why premarital sex is wrong. We need to be more creative than just telling them it is wrong. We need to help them understand sex from God's perspective—why He invented it and why it is the wise and righteous thing not to be involved with until you are with your lifelong partner in marriage.

CRISIS

The goal is for your teen to thoroughly understand the issues pertaining to sex, so she will have the moral strength to say "no"—not just because her parents said not to do it, but because she knows it is wrong and will mess her up.

When we say, "Don't ask why—just do it because I say so . . . and because the Bible says so," teens often rebel. They are not children anymore. They are young adults who want some understanding of *why*. Now it is time for you to become an expert of the *why* behind abstaining from sexual activity so you can share with your teen, not like a professor lecturing a student, but as a friend helping another friend.

Something has happened within your child as a result of her sexual activity. She is still your child, but in a sense, she has grown up and experienced a part of adulthood prematurely. As you try to help her understand the *whys*, it is important not to cram it down her throat, come off as "holier than thou," or act like you are trying to rescue her.

It is fine to express your disappointment in the *activity*, but don't express disappointment in *her*. Please make that clear. In fact, I would not even use the word "disappointment." Instead say, "I do not like your actions, but I still love you as a person." Then you can do some research and discuss the following:

CRISIS

Find health statistics. Sexual activity brings a huge risk of disease. Approximately one in four sexually active teens contracts an STD every year.[10] Tell your teen how many cases of venereal diseases are caught each year by teens, how many teens contract the AIDS virus each year, and what percent of condoms

It is fine to express your disappointment in the activity, but don't express disappointment in *her*.

do not work (which means that even if a condom is used, the teen can still give someone HIV or get someone pregnant). Having sex with someone is like having sex with all the partners he has had sex with in the last seven years. If any of them have HIV or any other sexually transmitted disease, she can contract it—even if her partner uses a condom.

Tell your young person statistics to let her know you care and that you know what you are talking about. One of the very reasons it is wrong—why God does not want sex outside of marriage—is because it is so easy to contract a disease. If you have just one life partner, it is impossible to contract these diseases.

Find pregnancy statistics. How many teenage girls get pregnant every year? How many girls have an abortion every year? Discuss the issue of messing up her life with a pregnancy, leading to difficult decisions about keeping the baby or giving it away or about being a father to a child. Everyone says, "It couldn't happen to me," but for nearly a million girls this year it has happened.[11] That means a million guys have had to face these issues as well, most of whom are not taking responsibility for their actions.

Discuss the media's influence. Thirty-three percent of 12- to 18-year-olds say the media influenced their decision to have sex, with more than half citing that their birth-control training came from television or the movies. More than half (53 percent) of teenage girls get their sex education from television and movies, and more

CRISIS

Restore a sense of pride and dignity in your teen. Let her know that even though she has made a mistake, she can walk purely from now on.

than one-third say fashion magazines are an important source of information about sex. One-third of all teenagers say the media encourages them to have sex. *Thirty-four percent say some teens have sex because television and movies make it seem normal.*[12]

First Corinthians 6:16 says, "Do you not know that he who unites himself with a prostitute is one with her in body?" "Is one with her" is a very strong statement. When your teen sexually unites with another person, she does not become one with them spiritually, but their souls have touched. They have experienced the greatest intimacy possible between two human beings. Something happens in her mind, will, and emotions—the three parts of her soul—they get connected. She has bared herself physically and emotionally before another person, which makes her vulnerable. The most personal, intimate part of her that anyone could ever know, someone now knows. Only one person should ever have the privilege of enjoying that very precious and private part of her.

Our society does not understand the value of intimacy. People are casually intimate with just about anyone, and it has lost its importance and value. Intimacy within marriage has become less valuable also. People's hearts, minds, wills, and emotions get profoundly confused and messed up when they continue to change sexual partners and fool around with anyone who comes along. They wonder why they feel empty, shallow, and hollow—unable to make commitments.

It is important you have her pray this to break that soul tie: "In Jesus' name, I refuse to allow this emotional attachment to this person to confuse and draw me away from God's best for my life."

Teach your young person about the preciousness of intimacy. Intimacy is not just sexual intercourse. She should not allow someone to touch any private parts of her body for any reason at any time. People say it is okay to fool around as long as you don't have sex. It is not! The privacy of her body should be reserved for the one person who has the courage and desire to commit his whole life to her—the person she marries. And only *after* the marriage ceremony. It is the gift God has given her to give to another person. Walking down the aisle on her wedding day, she wants to be able to say, "I have saved myself for you. Not just my virginity, but my privacy has been reserved for you, and I give myself to you." Teach your young person the value and honor of being pure.

Talk about a second virginity. What does this mean? *God cares more about the spirit of a virgin than the body of a virgin.* It is possible to say, "From this point on I am going to renew my commitment to purity before God. I am going to keep a pure heart and a pure body." Many people have messed up physically but through God's incredible grace, have a pure heart again.

Restore a sense of pride and dignity in your teen. Let her know that even though she has made a mistake, she can walk purely from now on. Walking down the aisle, she can still say, "I blew it when I was younger, but these past five years I have kept my heart, mind, and body pure, and I am ready to give myself to you." There is awesome virtue in that.

Begin an open dialogue with your teen, sharing honestly. Talk about what she should do if she is tempted, so as to ensure she doesn't accidentally slip into a compromising situation, such as being alone in the dark with a boy. You can find books in your local Christian bookstore that will give you wise guidance on the subject.

CRISIS

Some parents have bought a promise ring for their son or daughter. This ring is a symbol of his or her commitment to the Lord to remain pure until the day she is married. Remember, you don't want to simply tell her, "Stop doing it because I said so and because the Bible says so." The Bible is full of reasons *why*. As you give your teen biblical principles to stand on, she will be more willing to stand up and do the right thing.

God bless you as you instill godly values in your teen and help her get a renewed sense of purity and dignity about her future intimacy with her spouse.

chapter 19 Cutting: "It Only Hurts Me"

Much of this chapter is an adaptation of an article Jose Cano wrote in conjunction with Ron Luce's Teen Mania's Honor Academy, April 14, 2005.

Your daughter is locked in her bedroom, her eyes swollen with tears, struggling to express with words the turmoil she really feels deep down inside. In a bathroom stall, your son is hunched with hate and anger, overwhelmed with the constant reminder of his unbearable pain and looks for a way to get it out.

If you could see inside their souls, you would be surprised with what you'd find: confusion, torment, loneliness, numbness, hopelessness, hate, anger, and the list goes on. How can a parent help her teen out of the vicious cycle of spiritual, emotional, and physical abuse?

Cutting is a coping mechanism a young person has incorporated as a way of life in order to survive the emotional pain levels that may seem unbearable to him. The seriousness of the injuries will vary anywhere from heavily scratching of the skin to marks and lesions causing tissue damage severe enough to leave permanent scarring. Eventually, the teen may find herself cutting her body more consecutively and in more harmful ways.

The most common way teens "cut" are with razor blades, broken glass, or even writing utensils. The behavior often occurs sporadically and repetitively. *Oftentimes, it develops an "addictive" cycle and becomes an overwhelming preoccupation.*

If you suspect that your teen is cutting look for these signs:

- Lack of ability to express emotions verbally

- Lack of ability to handle intense feelings

- Perfectionism

- Severe mood swings

- A dislike for themselves and their bodies.

Some parents may think that cutting is part of a suicidal tendency, but suicide is not the end goal of cutting. Teens do not practice cutting with the intent to commit suicide or bring about sexual pleasure but for tension/emotional relief.

what to do

1. **To help and support your teen who may be "cutting," begin asking questions about what may be going on in her life that is leading her to use this method to relieve tension and stress.**
2. **Then begin to pray for your teen and talk to her about how she can find peace in her life.** *Help her acknowledge that Christ is our primary source of strength.* Pray with her, read the Bible together, and get her to an active youth ministry.
3. **Seek help from a youth pastor, counselor, or pastor to help her find a healthy way of coping.** Unless God does

If you could see inside their souls, you would be surprised with what you'd find: confusion, torment, loneliness, numbness, hopelessness, hate, anger, and the list goes on.

a miracle, it would be unrealistic to expect her to change her habit immediately. One thing is certain according to Romans 6:18: He has set us free, but it may be a process.

4. **Talk to her and hold her accountable.** If she comes to you to talk about the urge, it will help her reduce the distress of the moment. Therefore, help her build a network of godly friends and family that she can be honest with. They will support her during the difficult times. Above all, help her know that God is always there.

5. **Help her put new skills into practice.** In the past, whenever she felt the overwhelming sense of life's problems, she may have dealt with them through cutting. But, if she wants to stop hurting herself, it will be vital for her to start practicing new coping skills to overcome the urge to injure herself. Discuss with her some healthy alternatives to cutting. Be sure not to prescribe what she *should* do. Instead, dialogue with her, really listen and allow her to come up with coping ideas.

Photo © Big Cheese Photos

CRISIS

Christian T. Hill, a counselor who works extensively with teens, lists the following alterative coping strategies:

- Pray—God *will* give you the strength to resist temptation.

- Call a friend, youth pastor, parent, or crisis line.

- Try not to be alone (i.e. call up a friend and go shopping).

- Journal—write down all your positive points and why you deserve not to be hurt.

- Go for a walk or run (exercise can help relieve tension).

- Work with paint or clay.

- Listen to worship music.

- Cook or clean.

- Write a song about what you're feeling.[1]

Here are some questions that you can talk through with your teen. Be sure you have lots of time to listen. Help her to take time to answer them honestly. These questions will give you and your teen clues about the problems and issues you need to face and work on. And you can also seek out the help of a professional counselor to help you process these questions with your teen.

- Have I put my "new skills" into practice faithfully? Why do I feel I need to hurt myself?

- Have I been here before? What did I do to deal with it? How did I feel then?

She has to own the personal decision in order for change to start taking place. There is hope and a new way of living but your teen has to declare her own right to walk in freedom.

❧ What have I done to ease this discomfort so far? What else can I do that won't hurt me?

❧ What word(s) would I use to describe the feeling(s) I am experiencing right now?

❧ What do I tell myself or what do I hear my mind telling me during these times of struggle?

❧ What am I trying to say through my wounds?

❧ What does the pain I inflict on the outside say about the pain I feel in the inside?

❧ How do I feel about myself right now?

❧ How will I feel when I am hurting myself? (satisfied, angry, pleased, guilty, etc.)

❧ How will I feel after I hurt myself? (satisfied, angry, pleased, guilty, etc.) Was it worth it?

- ❖ How will I feel tomorrow morning? (satisfied, angry, pleased, guilty, etc.)

- ❖ How can I avoid this stressor or deal with it better in the future?

- ❖ Do I really need to hurt myself or is there something different I could have done to deal with my emotional pain?

- ❖ How close or distant do I feel to God before and after I hurt myself?

- ❖ What do I think Jesus feels about me hurting myself?

- ❖ What does He want me to remember during my times of temptation?

- ❖ How will I feel if I don't resist the temptation?

- ❖ How will I feel if I actually overcome this wave of temptation?

The decision to stop "cutting" is not an easy one for your teen to make. In order for her to be successful, the decision needs to come from her. *She has to own the personal decision in order for change to start taking place.* There is hope and a new way of living but your teen has to declare her own right to walk in freedom.

As this decision is made, it is beneficial for your teen, with your support, to set herself up to win. It will be a good idea to establish new boundaries and set guidelines to help the young person when she faces temptations that will lead her to old behavior.

In Him there is hope, life, and a new beginning. Therefore, it is vital to prepare our hearts and minds for action through His Word as we walk with our teen through this issue.

the christian walk

We as parents all long for our teens to have commitments to God and to church. Yet often, it is the last place they want to be.

"Christians are nerds."

"I feel like sleeping every time I sit in church."

Planting our teen in a church where he can have fun, grow in the Lord, and find his purpose should be a priority for every parent. How we do this will not be convenient or easy, but the long-term benefits will help our teen become the person God and we long for him to be.

chapter 20

Making Church Fun: A Place to Grow and Learn

It's Sunday morning and you begin the same conversation, trying to figure out new, creative ways to get your teenager to church.

Being a good parent, you demand that he goes no matter what. You don't know what else to do, but you figure if you can at least get him to church, maybe something good will sink in. You are taking the right action by making him go. Yet, is there a wiser way to accomplish the same objective or even a bigger objective?

teens and church

According to Nielsen Media Research study, the number one response about what kids like least about Christianity was *church*.[1]

> To their credit, teenagers are more focused on God than on the institutional church. Almost six out of ten of them say they want to be close to God; not quite four out of ten say they are anxious to be active participants in a church.... Half of all kids attend a church worship service each week. As might be expected, the older teenagers become, the less frequently they

attend church services, declining from two-thirds of all 13-year-olds attending church each weekend to less than half of all 18-year-olds. The most astounding realization in this regard is that teenagers are more likely to attend a church service every week than are adults. . . . It should not be surprising that most teens admit that the chances of their leaving the church are at least as good as the chances of staying. Only two out of every five teens (41 percent) say they are "very likely" to attend a church once they leave home. Roughly as many (36 percent) said they may attend, and the remaining one-quarter (22 percent) said the chances are slim to none.[2]

Most people who drop out of church do so between 16 and 19 years of age. The top six main reasons are:

1. Part-time jobs conflict with church life.
2. They think church is irrelevant.
3. They feel they don't fit in.
4. Challenging church training programs usually cease or taper off at this age.
5. Church activities are boring.
6. They are going through a time of questioning and doubting.[3]

Maybe you have felt frustrated trying to convey your faith, beliefs, and values to a teen. What are you to do? This should go without saying, but pray! Stand in the gap. Find Scriptures to stand on.

> *Train a child in the way he should go,*
> *and when he is old he will not turn from it.*
> —*Proverbs 22:6*

And afterward, I will pour out my Spirit on all people.
Your sons and daughters will prophesy, your old men
will dream dreams, your young men will see visions.
—Joel 2:28

All your sons will be taught by the Lord,
and great will be your children's peace.
—Isaiah 54:13

Pray those verses over your teen. Pray, "In Jesus' name, he is going to be God's person. Soften his heart, Lord." Pray that a passionate love for God will explode in his heart as the Lord becomes the center of everything he is.

Ask yourself, and do your best to discern from your teen, whether or not your young person really knows the Lord. The question is not really whether he likes church or not, but does he know the Lord? Has he ever given his life to Jesus?

"He has always been a good person . . . He doesn't really get into trouble . . ." But does he know the Lord? If he doesn't know the Lord, no wonder he thinks church and the Bible are boring. Talk to him. Through a series of conversations you will be able to tell if he knows the Lord. If he doesn't, spend your prayer time praying that he would truly, genuinely surrender to the Lord.

Find him a Bible that is easy to understand. It is amazing how many young people have King James Version Bibles or some other version they

Photo © Big Cheese Photos

THE CHRISTIAN WALK

do not understand. They get bored with it and do not read it any-more. Let me recommend to you a translation called the *Contemporary English Version*, a youth study Bible version that puts the Bible into today's language. The study aids will help your teen understand different passages of Scripture and give him insight on where to turn when he is struggling or challenged.

Ask yourself if the church you are going to is boring—maybe not for you, but is it for your teen? If you really want your teen on fire, you need to answer honestly. Maybe he is sincerely trying to get something out of it, but he can't because it's geared toward an older congregation. It may be providing a great social outlet for your family, but is your faith growing? More importantly, is your young person being presented the Gospel in such a way that will help him to grow in the Lord?

According to a survey of religious youth workers, more than nine in ten congregations say they have a problem with keeping high school students involved in church—compared to nine per-cent who say they are doing a good job reaching out to youth.[4] Inconsistency, irrelevance, independence, lack of other people their age, and school pressure are just a few reasons why kids turn away from church.[5]

We have always tried to get our chil-dren to read and feed their souls with Jesus. They go to youth group and choir and participate in hob-bies and sports. We try to keep the channel on family- or Christian-based content, and we try to keep up with the flood of garbage being fed to their young minds. So often it feels like a loosing battle. I have always taught my children that actions speak louder than words and that people will follow if you are righteous in your fight. So I must join the fight and show my

children by my actions how wrong and destructive the enemy's lies are for their minds and souls.
—Parent of a Teen

One reason teens and church may not mix well is that teens go unprepared. Most people have never been taught how to get something out of church. Another reason teens may resist church is because they aren't debriefed afterward. In other words, do we discuss at the table, "What went on at church? What did you think of the sermon? What are your questions?"[6]

This is a spiritual survival time, a matter of spiritual life or death for your young person! Do not play around and think, "Well, I like it, so he should like it too. It's good enough for me, so it's good enough for him." You can get fed through tapes, books, and seminars, but you have to go on a quest to find a place that has some real fire in their youth ministry—a place that will provide your young person with the greatest chance of catching the fire of God. Ask the Holy Spirit to lead you to the church you are supposed to belong to. Be open to His direction. Do not let your predisposition cloud your ability to see the truth.

Do not take chances with your young person. Do whatever it takes to get him in an environment where he loves church, youth group, and spending time in God's Word.

Do not take chances with your young person. Do whatever it takes to get him in an environment where he loves church, youth group, and spending time in God's Word.

Jay Kesler says, "An enterprising, middle-aged businessman has moved 23 times in their 35 years of marriage and yet has one of the most successful families going. When asked how he managed this, he responded with a real pearl of wisdom. 'Every time we moved to a new town,' he said, 'the first thing we did was look for a church with a program for kids the ages of ours. Then we found a house near it. We've been Methodists, Presbyterians, Episcopalians, Baptists, Assembly of God, and Free Churchmen. We've always felt that the key to helping our mobile family was to choose the church first, then the house.'"[7]

Once you find a place where your teen loves to go, do not use it as punishment. Do not prohibit him from going if he does something wrong. There are plenty of other things you can take away, but don't take away any kind of spiritual activity. You will be sending the wrong message. You think you are accomplishing the desired results because you are taking something away that he really loves. Do not take away anything that encourages love for God and use that against him as punishment.

chapter 21 Walking the Talk: Ministry Opportunities for Your Teen

There you are, trying to raise a teen who is responsible, doing all the right things with her life, going on to be a pillar in the community, and all of a sudden she comes home saying she wants to go on a mission trip. She wants to spend the summer in another nation where the people do not speak English, and *you* have never left the country yourself!

It's not as strange as you might think for your young person to want to do this. In fact, thousands of young people every year go on mission trips all around the world because God has touched their heart and given them a desire to go. It would be wise for us not to dismiss it as another teenage-hype experience, but to find out what we might do to encourage them to go.

God has laid missions on the hearts of young people all across the nation. Listen to what some teens have said:

"I said that I wanted to go on a mission trip two years ago. My parents told me they would pray about it and give me an answer. They never did, so I didn't go. Then I went to an ACQUIRE THE FIRE and God laid it on my heart to go to Bolivia. I told my parents

my decision and for some reason, they are now
holding a grudge against me. I am 17-years-old
and really have the desire to go on missions.
I know that it is God's will, but what do
I do about my parents?"

"I would just like some encouragement from my
parents about going on a mission trip."

"I want to go on a mission trip, but my parents
say that I need to get a summer job and
earn money for next year."

Go! I am sending you out like lambs among wolves.
—Luke 10:3

You ask, "Why go for just two weeks or just one or two months?
What good is that going to do?" Jesus sent His disciples out on
short-term trips, sometimes for a week, sometimes for a couple of
weeks. If Jesus sent His disciples on short-term trips, surely He
would know whether it is a valuable, credible way for a young person to spend her energy.

Sometimes we think, "Why does she need to go now? Why
don't they wait until she is older?" Jesus called His own disciples
lambs. They were not even sheep yet, they were lambs. They did

If your young person even
has even an inkling to go,
let her. You do not know if
the desire will always be there.
Seize the moment.

not know how to do very much. They were not very talented, and they asked a lot of stupid questions.

Maybe you feel your teen is too immature or not very strong in the Lord. Maybe she hasn't been a Christian very long. It is exactly that youthful zeal that Jesus wants to harness and use to change the world. The fact is an experience on the mission field during the teenage years could dramatically affect the way your teen spends the rest of her life. She can see God's hand directly involved in her life, using her to minister to people who have never heard about Jesus.

Photo © Photodisc

My 18-year-old daughter is a great example to her younger sisters. She just returned from the mission field. Praise God that we, as parents, did something right!

—*Parent of a Teen*

I know it is not easy to let go. While at a church where I was ministering, a man came up and grabbed my arm as I was getting ready to preach. He said,

Ron Luce, you came here a year ago and started talking about taking kids to Russia. I thought you were crazy. My daughter came home from church that day saying she wanted to go to Russia. I thought she was crazy. I told her I'd let her go if God would give her the money. God gave her the money, and I thought He was crazy. So last summer I let my little girl go to Russia. It was hard being away from her for two months, and I really had to use my faith to entrust her into God's hands. I got a couple postcards and a couple phone calls from her, but I was so excited to see her when she came home. I picked her up at the airport and as she was telling me all the stories of how God had used her, I thought

THE CHRISTIAN WALK

"Yeah, yeah, I'm just glad my baby is home." Then when we got to the house, we put in the video tape that showed my little girl involved in ministry.

This man began to cry, and with tears streaming down his face he said, "And when I saw my baby, my own flesh and blood, passing out tracts to those peo-ple who had never heard about Christ, I knew it was worth it. I knew it was worth entrusting her into the Lord's hands and it was worth all of the finances she had raised. I realized I had made a difference by sending my little girl."

If your young person even has even an inkling to go, let her. You do not know if the desire will always be there. Seize the moment. The older she gets, the more distractions there are—cars, clothes, jobs, and relationships.

Every summer, we at Teen Mania Ministries take thousands of teenagers on mission trips. We have seen literally hundreds of thousands of people won to the Lord as a result of young people reaching out with their faith. I have had countless parents tell me, "Thank you so much for doing in my young person what I could not do as a parent. I did everything I knew to do, but having her go on this mission trip completed everything!"

Do not be like that one parent who prayed, "Oh Lord, please do not let my young person go on a mission trip. I want her to be a success in life." The Lord wants to use her in a mighty way. Send her out to the mission field while she is young—it keeps her from getting into trouble in the summer, and it will plant in her heart a vision for God to use her for the rest of her life.

when your teen comes back

After he has come back from a camp, a conference, a mission trip, or an *Acquire the Fire* youth convention, he can't stop talking about what God did in his life. You have never seen anything like it! Now you just pray and hope that it stays.

Listen to what some teens have said:

> "I find it difficult to stay on fire for the Lord.
> I go to a pretty big church, but the
> youth group doesn't do anything."

> "It is hard to stay on fire when my parents
> say one thing, then do another. Their
> actions don't follow their words."

> "Many Christians I know are self-righteous
> and they are always right. I am losing interest
> in Christianity because most Christians
> I've met show more hatred than love."

> "I need more encouragement, discipline,
> and accountability from my parents
> particularly from my dad."

> "I always feel like I'm doing something
> wrong in my walk with God. I wish my
> parents would encourage me more."

> "I'm on a roller coaster ride with God. I can't
> keep focused. I have tried to, but when nothing
> happened, I kinda gave up for a while."

> "I wish my parents would encourage me
> instead of nagging me. I wish they wouldn't
> try to make me worship their way."

What can you do? Embrace your teen's excitement. Many parents patronize their young person. "Yeah, yeah, yeah. I remember when I was that fired up." They act as if their teen is excited over a new club or a new activity. Instead of patronizing your young person and playing down his newfound passion and love for Christ, embrace his fire.

Ask some questions about what God did. What specific things can you pray for? What is he going to do differently to make sure his fire does not die? What can you as a parent do to help him maintain his fire? He may have good suggestions for you. Ask what decisions he made during the camp, conference, or missions trip that he wants to be held accountable to.

Be a loving, concerned parent/friend who wants to be involved in your teen's life, embracing him, and genuinely believing God has changed his life. Listen to what your teen is sharing. This is the first step toward a lasting fervor for the Lord.

> *Never be lacking in zeal, but keep your spiritual fervor,*
> *serving the Lord.*
> *—Romans 12:11*

Keep *your* fire burning for God. Simply stated, do not keep a spiritual "air" about you without being truly spiritual. If you have areas of your walk with the Lord that are shallow or empty, deal with them. If you need to ask for someone's forgiveness and repent— then do it! Sometimes when we see our teen on fire, we get intimidated. We think, "What can he teach me that I haven't already

Keep *your* fire burning for God.

learned?" and we become guilty of the very thing he has been guilty of—sitting in the back of the church, acting like we've heard it all before.

A wise person can learn from anyone. Find time to spend on your knees before the Lord. Let it push you to deeper levels of humility, deeper levels of intimacy with God, and more passionate times in reading and meditating on His Word. You'll enter new realms of fasting, praying, and staying on your knees until you hear the voice of God.

Start having honest discussions with your teen regarding your Christian life and his Christian life. Do not try to be pseudo-spiritual, which your teen will interpret as fake, but seek God with more fervor than you ever have. If your young person is going after the Lord with all he's got, you have to go after Him even harder to provide spiritual leadership. As you share your prayer concerns, struggles, and victories in your walk with the Lord, your young person will do the same with you. You will be on the road to a discipling relationship with your young person. But do not assume that now that he is on fire for God, he will stay that way forever. That fire must continually be fanned and encouraged in order for it to be kept burning.

In the process of establishing this type of dialogue, let there be some mutual accountability. Ask your teen to hold you accountable to having quiet times or to dealing with certain areas of your life—not so he can throw it in your face later, but so you can show a little trust and respect. Then ask him, "How can I pray for you? What challenges do you have that you want God to help you get through?"

Photo © Photodisc

THE CHRISTIAN WALK

Help your teen find what that next mountain is. Help him define the next step in his spiritual journey.

A fallacy many parents buy into is thinking we need to keep our young person on that spiritual mountaintop. We want him to stay there forever and hope it never goes away. First of all, you cannot just hope—you must do something to keep the fire burning. Do not presume he will accidentally stay on fire forever.

There is not supposed to be just one mountaintop. We are supposed to go back again and again into the presence of God. We are not supposed to hope our young person stays on that mountain but that he gets taken to the next mountain.

What's the next challenge in his life? What's the next area God wants him to grow in? Maybe it's another mission trip or camp. Maybe it's doing ministry in the inner city. Maybe there are areas of his character God wants to refine. Ask the question, "Why did God give you that fire and what is the next mountain God wants you to climb?"

Help your teen find what that next mountain is. Help him define the next step in his spiritual journey. He needs to feel support and guidance. You cannot just depend on your pastor and youth pastor. Be the spiritual leader of your home! Help your young person see that he has the fire for a reason. God wants to do something in him and through him.

Finding Their Purpose: Now What?

chapter 22

Where there is no vision, the people perish . . .
—Proverbs 29:18 KJV

Without a vision, the people are destroyed, aimless, confused, bewildered, and directionless. This describes much of what this generation of young people is like.

> "I didn't have a job, so my mom just yelled at me
> and told me I was lazy and would never get a job."

> "My parents need to encourage me
> and tell me to press on with my goals."

Many parents feel sad that their own teen does not have direction, but they don't quite know what to do about it. They figure that somehow, some way, their young person will figure out what she should do with her life. She graduates from high school and goes through one door at a time to find her way in life. Seventeen-year-old Brooke Davidoff said, "About one-third of our generation doesn't care about anything important. It's kind of like anything goes."[1] "More than 98 percent of teens ages 13 to 17 say it's at least somewhat likely that they will have good-paying jobs as adults, and more than six in ten think that there is some likelihood they may be rich someday. Yet almost half say they are likely to be mugged, and 33 percent believe they may be shot or stabbed in their lifetime."[2]

the importance of goals (for you and your teen)

According to a 1999 poll of teenagers, 87.2 percent indicated that personal goals as "very" or "somewhat" important in pursuing a specific job or career. For gaining entrance into a financially attractive career, 80.7 percent agreed. Being with friends was an important influence at 78.9 percent, developing a creative ability/talent was at 77.6 percent, and learning more about subjects that have interested me in high school was 75.5 percent.[3]

As a parent, one of our goals should be to raise our children to be morally and socially responsible so they will do the right thing even without our supervision. Part of raising a responsible young person is helping her to know what to do with her life and helping to sort out the myriad of options.

Some parents want their children to live out their dreams. So they have always told their young person, "You are going to be a doctor," or "You are going to be a lawyer." Setting aside all of our personal biases and opinions, we need to look at our teen's utmost good and help her discover what God's plan is for *her* life. If *we*

You must remember, though, that it is her life, not yours. We should help her discover her dreams and develop a vision for her life.

never sought to find God's will for *our* life when we were young, this can be frustrating for us. Some of us struggle to find out what the Lord wants us to do now.

Your teen actually wants you to be involved in helping her discover what is right for her life. As one teen put it,

> **"I wish my parents cared about what
> I wanted to do with my life, but they
> keep trying to kill my dreams."**

Whatever you do, be careful not to be a dream-killer. Many parents have discouraged their young person by things they have said. The teen will mention an idea, and her parents will respond with, "Oh, you will never do that," "You can never become that," or "You will probably be flipping burgers your whole life." *Even though these things may be said in jest, the damage they can do to a young person's dreams is not only destructive but often eternal.* Without a doubt, as you begin to talk to your teen about her desires and dreams for the future, she will come up with ideas and dreams that might sound farfetched, way beyond her ability, or way beyond your desire for her to go that direction. You must remember, though, that it is *her* life, not yours. We should help her discover her dreams and develop a vision for her life.

Another equally important goal is to help your young person find out what God's best is for her life. Many people have never considered what God's plan might be. Yet there is something about important decisions like what college to go to and who to marry that makes everyone wonder, "Is this really the right thing?" You can only measure whether it is right or not by knowing the One who made you and knowing all the potential He put inside you.

Before I formed you in the womb I knew you, before you were born I set you apart; I appointed you as a prophet to the nations.
—Jeremiah 1:5

Before we were ever conceived, God knew who we were, what our gifts were going to be, all the potential He put inside of us, all the incredible things each of us could do to change the world and make it a better place.

Our responsibility is to help our young person realize the destiny and potential God has placed in her life. We, and our teen, need to open our ears and hearts to hear what God's plan is.

The first step in knowing His plan is knowing Him. If you want to know the purpose for a piano, go talk to the one who made the piano. He will tell you why he made it and its use. If we want to know the purpose of our lives, we need to go to our Maker and find out His plan for us.

Tom East, in *Vision and Challenge*, points out three ways you can enable young people to hear God's voice more clearly in their noisy world.

1. **Media literacy.** Professional attention-getters bombard teenagers with constant messages. When you help kids critique the media world in which they live, they're better able to understand these influences and the choices they present. This can help them focus on God's call.

2. **Reflection.** Teenagers need space to reflect on the direction their lives are taking. Silence is an important part of learning to pay attention. You can help kids by building pauses and short periods of silence into programs. Be sure to help them make connections between their beliefs and their actions.

3. **A spiritually challenging vision of life.** Give teenagers lots of opportunities to see God's call lived out in others' lives. Communicate a broad vision to kids by introducing them to a variety of people who are living for Christ in everyday life.[4]

During this process, help your young person make a list of all her gifts and talents, all the things she has ever wanted to do with her life, and all the ideas and opinions others have had regarding what she should do with her life (i.e. fields that people have suggested she should go into). Most importantly, help your young person discover her own convictions.

God has deposited convictions in our own hearts and lives, and we often do not search deep inside enough to know what those are. A conviction is something you feel so strongly about that if you do not do it, you know you will be miserable for the rest of your life. You can have convictions such as, "I must work in the medical field," "I must help people in some way," or "I must work in another country as a missionary."

Begin a dialogue with your young person. Discuss these kinds of things with her and meet once a month during the high school years to add or delete to the list. You will see how things are refined after a number of years or months of going through this kind of process.

Spend time praying over each item on the list. Consider talking to people who are experts in some of the areas your young

A conviction is something you feel so strongly about that if you do not do it, you know you will be miserable for the rest of your life.

THE CHRISTIAN WALK

If your teen does have a vision of what he wants to do, the first question to ask regarding a college would be, "Where is the best place for him to go to become an expert in this area?"

person is interested in. By letting your young person know you are interested and helping her walk through the milieu of confusion and options she is facing will show you care.

To reinforce her sense of purpose and destiny, help your teen write down her vision for life.

Write down the revelation [vision] and make it plain on tablets so that a herald may run with it.
—Habakkuk 2:2

After seeking and thinking through all the different possibilities, it is very important to have your young person write down a mini-plan. "This is where I'm going and this is how I'm going to get there" is the essence of this plan.

In a study of Harvard graduates, only three percent had written down their vision when they graduated. After 10 years, only that three percent had accomplished their vision and each were making an annual salary that averaged 10 times as much as the other 97 percent of graduates all together![5] Realize the importance of writing down your vision!

choosing a college

It stands to reason that if a teen desires to go to college, he should first have an idea of the direction he wants to go.

So many teens struggle with the decision of what college to go to.

THE CHRISTIAN WALK

"It seems as though I have too many options. With
so many options, it is hard for me to choose."

"I wish we would have started planning for college
or praying about it earlier. I feel like I don't know
where God would want me to go or to do."

"I wish my parents would say, 'Let God be
your guide, not money or your own mind-set.
God has a greater plan for you.'"

If your teen does have a vision of what he wants to do, the first
question to ask regarding a college would be, "Where is the best
place for him to go to become an expert in this area?" Research
schools that would best equip them, regardless of finances. Some
characteristics college freshmen say were very important in
helping them select the college they now attend are:

- ❖ Good academic reputation: 56.1 percent

- ❖ Graduates get good jobs: 47.5 percent

- ❖ Graduates go to top graduate schools: 27.5 percent

- ❖ Good social reputation: 26.7 percent

- ❖ Special programs: 22 percent

- ❖ Low tuition: 20.9 percent

- ❖ Financial assistance: 20.2 percent

- ❖ Proximity to home: 17.9 percent[6]

Begin researching various schools. Look at degree plans at the university your teen is considering. What classes would your teen be required to take? Study those classes to see what they would actually learn by taking them, not just what the title of the classes are.

Graduates should be able to share what they got out of their program. Talk to current students as well. College is like a greenhouse or an incubator in terms of attitude and probability for success. What is the *environment* of the campus?

Some might say, "Why go to college? Is everyone designed for college?" Jesus said in Luke 14:28–30, "Suppose one of you wants to build a tower. Will he not first sit down and estimate the cost to see if he has enough money to complete it? For if he lays the foundation and is not able to finish it, everyone who sees it will ridicule him, saying, 'This fellow began to build and was not able to finish.'"

The same is true of your young person's vision. He has these great visions, dreams, and goals, yet he has not realized what it takes to fulfill them.

Finding the right college is like counting the cost in building a tower. It is the preparation in order for the tower to stand. What environment will thrust them to the front lines of excellence?

If your teen gets to the end of high school and does not yet know what he wants to do, instead of stumbling through a year of college trying to figure it out or just working for a year, he ought to enlist in a program that can develop his future and potential. Getting involved in a program such as the Teen Mania Internship can be most beneficial. Hundreds of young people come every year for a whole year to develop character and vision for life. You can find more information about the internship program by logging onto **www.teenmania.com** or writing to: Teen Mania Ministries, P.O. Box 2000, Garden Valley, TX, 75771-2000.

> *Commit to the LORD whatever you do,*
> *and your plans will succeed.*
> *—Proverbs 16:3*

By walking down this road with your young person, you hope to see him launch into the direction in life he is best suited for. You can watch him accomplish all the dreams God has placed in his heart and become a success in whatever field he is destined to go into.

endnotes

Chapter 1

1 Jay Kesler, *Ten Mistakes Parents Make With Teenagers* (Brentwood, TN: Wolgemuth & Hyatt, 1988).

2 Kathleen McCoy, Ph.D., AGS Publishing, "Teen Rebellion: What's Normal, What's Not," **www.agsnet.com/parenting/nov04a.asp** (accessed December 6, 2005).

3 James Dobson, *Parenting Isn't for Cowards* (Dallas, TX: Word, 1996), 145.

4 Josh McDowell, *Josh McDowell's Handbook on Counseling Youth* (Dallas, TX: Word, 1996), 235–236.

5 *USA Today*, March 26, 1996.

6 George Barna, *Generation Next* (Ventura, CA: Regal, 1997), 100.

7 Ibid.

8 Ibid.

9 Ibid., 101.

10 *GROUP Magazine*, March 1994, 29.

Chapter 2

1 James Dobson, *Parenting Isn't for Cowards*, 164–165.

2 Jay Kesler with Ronald A. Beers, eds., *Parents and Teenagers* (Colorado Springs, CO: Victor, 1984), 118.

[3] James Dobson, *Parenting Isn't for Cowards*.

[4] David Blankenhorn, *Fatherless America: Confronting Our Most Urgent Social Problem* (New York, NY: Harper Perennial, 1996).

[5] *Newsweek*, June 17, 1996.

[6] *Reader's Digest*, February 1997, p. 65.

[7] Mike Yorkey, ed., *The Christian Family Answer Book*, 42.

[8] William Beausay II, *Boys! Shaping Ordinary Boys into Extraordinary Men* (Nashville, TN: Thomas Nelson, 1994).

Chapter 4

[1] *Smart Money*, September 1995.

[2] *Josh McDowell's Handbook on Counseling Youth*, 197–206.

[3] David R. Miller, *Counseling Families After Divorce*, 220.

Chapter 5

[1] Eugene C. Roehlkepartain, ed., *The Youth Ministry Resource Book* (Loveland, CO: Group Books, 1988), 37.

[2] *TeenAge Magazine*.

[3] Jay Kesler with Ronald A. Beers, eds., *Parents and Teenagers*, 359.

[4] Ibid.

Chapter 6

[1] The Alan Guttmacher Institute, "Patterns of Contraception Use Within Teenagers' First Sexual Relationships," (CPYU's Youth Culture Update #51) January 14, 2004.

Chapter 7

[1] "How to Tell If You're a Lesbian," "How to Tell Your Parents If You Are a Lesbian," and "How to Have Safe Lesbian Sex." *Seventeen*, June 2005.

"Culture" Section Division Page

[1] Ron Luce, *Battle Cry for a Generation* (Colorado Springs, CO: Cook Communications Ministries, 2005), 30.

Chapter 8

1 Quentin J. Schultze, *Winning Your Kids Back From the Media.*

2 James Dobson and Gary Bauer, *Children at Risk* (Dallas, TX: Word, 1994), 65.

3 Ibid., 213.

Chapter 9

1 *1987 Nielsen Report on Television*, Nielsen Media Research, 1987, 6–9.

2 "What Our Kids Think," *USA Today,* May 26, 1987, 6D.

3 *The Brown University Child and Adolescent Behavior Letter*, May 1995.

4 To find statistics like this—and many others—go to such Web sites as: **www.parentstv.org**; **www.frc.org**; or **www.clickz.com/stats/sectors/demographics**.

5 Quentin J. Schultze, *Winning Your Kids Back From the Media*, 122.

6 *The Columbia*, South Carolina State, February 7, 1996.

7 George Barna, *Generation Next* (Ventura, CA: Regal, 1997).

8 James Dobson and Gary Bauer, *Children at Risk*, 207.

9 *The Denver Post*, August 22, 1995.

10 *The Brown University Child and Adolescent Behavior Letter*, May 1995.

Chapter 10

1 J. Mitchell Kimberly, et. al., "The exposure of youth to unwanted sexual material on the Internet." *Youth and Society*, Vol. 34 No.3, March 2003, 330-358.

2 Judith Reisman, *Soft Porn Plays Hard Ball: Its Tragic Effects on Women, Children and the Family* (Lafayette, LA: Huntington House, 1991).

3 "Pornography Statistics 2003," Family Safe Media.

4 Ibid.

5 Judith Reisman, *Soft Porn Plays Hard Ball: Its Tragic Effects on Women, Children and the Family.*

Chapter 12

1 Suicide Deaths, U.S. 2001. **http://familyfirstaid.org/suicide.html**.

2 The Nation's Voice on Mental Illness, "Teenage Suicide," **www.nami.org/Content/ContentGroups.Helpline1/Teenage_Suicide.htm** (accessed November 14, 2005).

3 American Foundation for Suicide Prevention, "When You Fear Someone May Take Their Life," **http://www.afsp.org/index-1.htm** (accessed November 14, 2005).

Chapter 13

1 James Dobson, *Love Must Be Tough: New Hope for Families in Crisis* (Sisters, OR: Multnomah, 2004).

Chapter 14

1 Elizabeth A. Yeater and William O'Donohue, "Sexual Assault Prevention Programs: Current Issues, Future Directions, and the Potential Efficacy of Interventions with Women," *Clinical Psychology Review*, Vol. 19, No. 7, 739.

2 *San Diego Union-Tribune*, September 1995.

3 Ibid.

4 Jeanette D. Gardner, "Dispelling the Myths."

5 Jay Kesler with Ronald A. Beers, eds., *Parents and Teenagers*, 510–511.

Chapter 15

1 *New York Times*, December 13, 1994.

2 Greater Dallas Council on Alcohol and Drug Abuse, "Marijuana," **www.gdcada.org/statistics/marijuana.htm** (accessed December 6, 2005).

3 Healthmoon, "Marijuana Statistics," **www.geocities.com/health-moon/smoking-marijuana/stats.htm** (accessed December 6, 2005).

4 Ibid.

5 *Josh McDowell's Handbook on Counseling Youth*, 401.

6 *USA Today*, October 22, 1996.

[7] *Josh McDowell's Handbook on Counseling Youth*, 401–402.

[8] *GROUP Magazine*, September/October 1996, 16.

[9] Lucas Stang. "Drugs: Talking with Your Teen," ETR Associates, 2002 (distributed 2005 by McMaster Center for Alcohol and Drug Treatment, El Paso County Department of Health and Environment, Colorado Springs, CO).

Chapter 16

[1] Jay Kesler with Ronald A. Beers, eds., *Parents and Teenagers*, 501.

[2] American Lung Association. **www.lungusa.org/site/pp.asp? c-c/lluk900e&b=39868**

[3] American Cancer Society. **www.cancer.org/docroot/ped/content/ped-10-2x-smokeless_tobacco_and_cancer.asp**

Chapter 17

[1] *Who's Who Among American High School Students*, 1996.

[2] "Did You Know," **www.madd.org/stats/o,,1056,1789,00.html**.

Chapter 18

[1] The Alan Guttmacher Institute, "Patterns of Contraception Use Within Teenagers' First Sexual Relationships," January 14, 2004.

[2] National Campaign to Prevent Teen Pregnancy (True Lies e-mail update), January 2004.

[3] *San Diego Union-Tribune/USA Today*, June 25, 1996.

[4] *Josh McDowell's Handbook on Counseling Youth*.

[5] *GROUP Magazine*, November/December 1996.

[6] Mike Yorkey, ed., *The Christian Family Answer Book*, 237–238.

[7] As reported by the Center for Parent/Youth Understanding, quoted in the article in *AFA Journal*, January 14, 2004.

[8] Surveys conducted by the Kaiser Family Foundation and Seventeen magazine, reported in the article by *AFA Journal*, January 14, 2005.

[9] National Campaign to Prevent Teen Pregnancy (True Lies E-mail Update), January 2004.

[10] Kaiser Family Foundation, **www.kff.org**.

[11] "Teen Pregnancy Statistics," **http:www.ovenbuns.com/3d-ultra-sound-articles/teen-pregnancy.htm** (accessed November 15, 2005).

[12] **San Diego Union-Tribune/USA TODAY**, June 25, 1996; Chicago Tribune, July 9, 1996.

Chapter 19

[1] Christian T. Hill, MA. Alpine Connection, information presented at the "Issues Facing Teens" seminar at Pine Creek High School, Colorado Springs, CO, November 8, 2005.

Chapter 20

[1] *GROUP Magazine*, September/October 1996.

[2] George Barna, *Generation Next*, 80.

[3] Ibid.

[4] *The State Newspaper*, Spring 1996.

[5] Jay Kesler with Ronald A. Beers, eds., *Parents and Teenagers*, 367.

[6] Ibid., 371.

[7] Ibid., 367.

Chapter 22

[1] *Parade Magazine*, November 10, 1996.

[2] George H. Gallup International Institute survey.

[3] "Personal Goals Influencing Future Plans," **http://www.edu.gov.mb.ca/researchreports/transitions/section3**, 1999.

[4] *GROUP Magazine*, February 1996.

[5] Patsi Krafoff, Psy.D., CBC. *Customized Newsletter Services*, "The Art of the Goal: (Part 1) Are you Part of the 3 Percent," 2004, **http://www.customizednewsletters.com/featured/art_of_goal_1.html** (accessed November 15, 2005).

[6] Alexander W. Astin, Kenneth C. Green, William S. Korn and Marilynn Schalit, *The American Freshman: National Norms for Fall 1987* (Los Angeles, CA: Higher Education Research Institute, Graduate School of Education, University of California, December 1987) 50, 58.

The Word at Work Around the World

A vital part of Cook Communications Ministries is our international outreach, Cook Communications Ministries International (CCMI). Your purchase of this book, and of other books and Christian-growth products from Cook, enables CCMI to provide Bibles and Christian literature to people in more than 150 languages in 65 countries.

Cook Communications Ministries is a not-for-profit, self-supporting organization. Revenues from sales of our books, Bible curricula, and other church and home products not only fund our U.S. ministry, but also fund our CCMI ministry around the world. One hundred percent of donations to CCMI go to our international literature programs.

CCMI reaches out internationally in three ways:

· Our premier International Christian Publishing Institute (ICPI) trains leaders from nationally led publishing houses around the world.

· We provide literature for pastors, evangelists, and Christian workers in their national language.

· We reach people at risk—refugees, AIDS victims, street children, and famine victims—with God's Word.

Word Power, God's Power

Faith Kidz, RiverOak, Honor, Life Journey, Victor, NexGen — every time you purchase a book produced by Cook Communications Ministries, you not only meet a vital personal need in your life or in the life of someone you love, but you're also a part of ministering to José in Colombia, Humberto in Chile, Gousa in India, or Lidiane in Brazil. You help make it possible for a pastor in China, a child in Peru, or a mother in West Africa to enjoy a life-changing book. And because you helped, children and adults around the world are learning God's Word and walking in his ways.

Thank you for your partnership in helping to disciple the world. May God bless you with the power of his Word in your life.

For more information about our international ministries, visit www.ccmi.org.

The Devozine
Teens are Flipping Over!

8.5 x 10.875 • 96 pages

Teens everywhere are getting into the *Acquire the Fire* devotional magazine—half for girls, half for guys. It hits teens right where they live—in the language they understand. It talks about the issues that they deal with and that are important to them. And most importantly it puts the life of teens in perspective, reminding them what God thinks, how He wants them to live, and why it's important to them—now and for the rest of their lives.

Each quarterly issue offers 40 devos, plus music reviews, articles by teens and youth leaders, real-life faith stories, quizzes, teen-to-teen wisdom and Top 10 lists.

Also Available!
Companion Discussion Guide for Youth Workers and Parents

A separate Discussion Guide is available for YOU so you can use the *Acquire the Fire Teen Devotional* as an alternative curriculum with your youth group. The Guide provides 10, 15-20 minute lessons. Use it for any occasion you can think of!

Create an Explosion of Growth and Energy in Your Youth Ministry!

REVOLUTION YM
The Complete Guide to High-Impact Youth Ministry

Based on the proven experience of youth minister Ron Luce, this is the comprehensive guide to high-impact, vital youth ministry! Designed to help youth leaders grow their ministries in effectiveness and in numbers. Care is taken in helping leaders establish a youth ministry philosophy, and by providing inspiration and step-by-step plans to help them make their ministry vision a reality!

ISBN: 0-78144-302-4 • Item #104507
Hardcover with CD • 6x9 • 480 pages

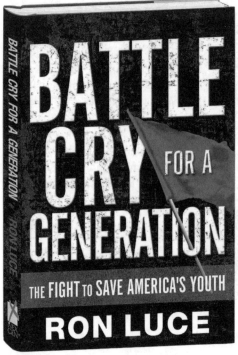